Discovering Existential Intelligence:
Tools, Insights, and Implications

Flávia Ceccato

TABLE OF CONTENT

Dedication

To my beloved children, Marcéu and Isis,

May you always seek meaning beyond the ordinary, question with curiosity, and embrace the wonder of existence.

This book is a reflection of the journey to understand life's deepest questions. I hope it inspires you to explore your purpose, connect with the world around you, and cultivate wisdom that goes beyond knowledge.

May you walk your path with an open mind, a courageous heart, and the certainty that you are deeply loved.

With all my love,

Flávia Ceccato

Acknowledgments

The journey of writing *Discovering Existential Intelligence: Tools, Insights, and Implications* has been an enlightening and deeply rewarding experience, and I owe immense gratitude to those who have supported and inspired me along the way.

To my family, friends, and mentors who have guided and challenged me throughout this process. Your wisdom and encouragement have been invaluable. Thank you for inspiring me to ask deeper questions, seek greater truths, and embrace the infinite journey of learning.

I also wish to thank Professor Howard Gardner for his openness to dialogue and for generously answering my questions throughout this journey.

With deep appreciation,

Flávia Ceccato

About the Author

Flávia Ceccato is a Federal Auditor of External Control at the Brazilian Federal Court of Accounts, with over 15 years of experience in public auditing, regulatory evaluation, and oversight of complex infrastructure sectors.

Her distinguished multidisciplinary academic background includes bachelor's degrees in Architecture and Physics, a master's degree in Regulation and Business Management, and postgraduate specializations in ABA Intervention for Autism and Intellectual Disability, Astronomy Teaching, and Spirituality and Consciousness Studies. This combination of technical, scientific, behavioral, and philosophical training underpins her signature approach: integrating analytical rigor, human cognition, and systemic thinking to produce innovative solutions. She is also a sought-after international keynote speaker, routinely invited to conferences globally.

Beyond her professional accomplishments, she is an active member of prestigious high-IQ societies such as Mensa, the International Society for Philosophical Enquiry (ISPE), and Intertel. Her commitment to advancing audit methodologies is reflected in numerous scientific and technical publications, particularly her groundbreaking work applying Benford's Law to enhance transparency and accuracy in public audits. She received a record for this pioneering work in Brazil, certified by RankBrasil.

Introduction

Have you ever stared at the stars and wondered about the meaning of life? Or maybe you've contemplated why we're here while waiting for your coffee to brew. Congratulations! You've just dabbled in existential intelligence, a form of intelligence that's all about pondering life's big questions, like "What is my purpose?" and "When we die, do we go somewhere else, or do we cease to exist?" This study is here to prove that such musings are more than just late-night brain gymnastics; they're an essential aspect of human cognition.

This work aims to propose a comprehensive framework for measuring existential intelligence by refining and deepening its conceptual domains, emphasizing its profound significance for humanity. Right now, the academic world is scratching its collective head over how to define existential intelligence, with some researchers mistakenly lumping it together with spiritual intelligence. Spoiler alert: they're not the same thing. Clarifying these distinctions isn't just a theoretical exercise; it's the key to unlocking new insights into how we think about existence itself.

Existential intelligence, as conceptualized within Howard Gardner's theory of multiple intelligences, is essentially the "deep thinker" of the family. It's the sibling that sits quietly at the dinner table, pondering the meaning of the universe while everyone else argues about dessert. This intelligence involves engaging with the big, hairy questions of life, death, and our place in the grand scheme of things. While everyone might occasionally wonder if we're just Sims in someone else's game, truly honing existential intelligence requires a unique set of cognitive and emotional skills—skills this study seeks to explore and measure.

Why does this matter, you ask? Well, existential intelligence isn't just about impressing people at dinner parties. It has major implications for the study of human consciousness. Imagine being able to measure this form of intelligence accurately. We could unlock correlations between existential intelligence and IQ, discover how it intersects with altered states of consciousness, and even figure out why some people can stay calm during existential crises while others spiral into a weeklong Netflix binge.

Currently, the tools we use to measure existential intelligence are a bit like trying to play Mozart on a kazoo—they're not quite hitting the mark. Many of them mix existential intelligence with spiritual intelligence or fail to capture its nuances. This study is here to fix that by proposing a clearer, more targeted approach to understanding this fascinating domain. Think of it as upgrading from a flip phone to a smartphone—a leap forward in precision and capability.

But wait, there's more! Beyond psychometric tests, existential intelligence has enormous potential in education. Picture classrooms where students don't just memorize facts but engage with questions like, "What gives life meaning?" and "How can I contribute to the world?" By integrating existential intelligence into curricula, educators could foster critical thinking, emotional resilience, and a deeper sense of purpose in students. Let's face it: these skills are way more useful than knowing how to diagram a sentence (no offense to grammar enthusiasts).

Now let's talk about modern life. We're living in a world so chaotic that we've coined not one but two acronyms to describe it: VUCA (Volatility, Uncertainty, Complexity, Ambiguity) and BANI (Brittle, Anxious, Nonlinear, Incomprehensible). In these turbulent times, existential intelligence is like a compass in a storm. It helps us find meaning, stay grounded, and navigate through life's curveballs without losing our sanity. Whether it's dealing with climate change, pandemics, or the mystery of why socks disappear in the laundry, this intelligence is a survival skill for the modern era.

Finally, let's not forget the interdisciplinary magic of existential intelligence. By combining insights from psychology, neuroscience, philosophy, and education, this study paints a holistic picture of how we grapple with life's big questions. Whether it's drawing on ancient philosophical traditions or the latest brain imaging studies, this work bridges the gap between deep thought and empirical science.

In conclusion, this study doesn't just aim to measure existential intelligence—it seeks to celebrate it. By addressing gaps in the literature and proposing better tools for understanding this intelligence, we hope to inspire a world where pondering life's mysteries is seen as a strength, not a quirk. So, the next time you find yourself staring at the stars, remember: you're not just daydreaming. You're engaging in one of humanity's most profound forms of intelligence—and that's something worth measuring.

Redefining Human Potential From IQ to Existential Mastery

The Evolution of Intelligence:

From IQ to Multiple Intelligences

Until the end of the last century, intelligence was viewed through a very specific lens—one that came with a lot of test sheets, No. 2 pencils, and the looming dread of an IQ score. The classical psychometric view of intelligence predominated, defining intelligence as the ability to answer test items designed to measure one's intelligence quotient (IQ). Essentially, intelligence was seen as a "one-size-fits-all" cognitive ability, conveniently squeezed into a number. Statistical techniques supported this view, comparing responses from individuals of different ages to infer some mysterious underlying skill—as if intelligence were a universal standard like the boiling point of water. Simple, right?

Enter Howard Gardner. In the late 1970s and early 1980s, this revolutionary psychologist took one look at the classical concept of intelligence and said, "Nope, humans are way more complicated than that." Thus, the theory of multiple intelligences was born. Gardner proposed that intelligence was not some monolithic ability but rather a diverse array of cognitive skills that people use to solve problems and create meaningful contributions to their societies. Essentially, he expanded the view of intelligence from "Can you solve this math problem?" to "Can you play a symphony, inspire a crowd, or navigate a forest?"

Gardner's (1983, 1999) theory identified eight distinct intelligences: linguistic intelligence, logical-mathematical intelligence, spatial intelligence, musical intelligence, bodily-kinesthetic intelligence, naturalistic intelligence, interpersonal intelligence, and intrapersonal intelligence. Suddenly, intelligence was no longer confined to acing tests or solving equations; it included the ability to dance, paint, connect with others, or even understand oneself deeply. Finally, a theory that acknowledged the chess prodigy and the virtuoso violinist as just as intelligent as the calculus whiz. Revolutionary!

According to Gardner, modern secular schools have been guilty of playing favorites, valuing only two intelligences: linguistic and logical-mathematical. This duo, dubbed "academic intelligence," hogs the spotlight in classrooms around the globe. Sure, being able to write essays and solve algebraic equations is important, but Gardner argued that these skills barely scratch the surface of what humans are capable of. It's like judging a fish on its ability to climb a tree—you're missing out on a whole ocean of talent!

Gardner's idea of multiple intelligences marked a radical departure from the traditional notions of intelligence that dominated the early 20th century. These older models, popularized by psychologists like Piaget (1950, 1952), focused heavily on cognitive development and IQ tests as the gold standard for intelligence.

Gardner's theory flipped the script, inviting a more inclusive view of human potential that resonated across disciplines.

What makes Gardner's theory even more compelling is how he arrived at it. Unlike traditional psychologists who were preoccupied with creating and interpreting psychometric instruments, Gardner drew from a kaleidoscope of research fields—evolutionary biology, neuroscience, anthropology, psychometrics, and psychological studies of prodigies and savants. His holistic approach allowed him to identify a set of criteria that distinguished one intelligence from another, moving beyond test scores to uncover the rich tapestry of human abilities.

Gardner's observation of real-world talent played a pivotal role in shaping his theory. He noted that individuals with extraordinary skills in domains like chess, music, athletics, politics, or entrepreneurship demonstrated cognitive abilities that couldn't be shoehorned into a narrow definition of intelligence. These talents, he argued, deserved to be recognized and celebrated as legitimate forms of intelligence. Essentially, Gardner reminded the world that intelligence is as diverse as humanity itself—and that's a beautiful thing.

In summary, the theory of multiple intelligences challenged the traditional psychometric view of intelligence, moving beyond the rigid confines of IQ testing. By expanding the definition of intelligence to include a broader range of human abilities, Gardner's work revolutionized how we think about learning, talent, and human potential. So the next time you find yourself inspired by a dancer, a scientist, or a master gardener, remember: intelligence isn't just one thing—it's many, and it's everywhere.

Existential Intelligence: The "8½" Intelligence that Keeps us Asking "Why?"

Over the years, Gardner's theory of multiple intelligences has inspired an ever-growing list of contenders for "new intelligences," ranging from moral intelligence to humorous intelligence and even culinary intelligence (because who doesn't admire a chef who can whip up Michelin-starred existential comfort food?). Among these, Gardner himself flirted with the idea of **existential intelligence**—a cognitive ability that reflects humanity's knack for tackling the Big Questions: *Why are we here? Why do we love? Why do we die?*

Gardner (2006a) proposed **existential intelligence** as the ability to contemplate fundamental aspects of human existence—questions about life, death, reality, and our ultimate purpose. Imagine the mental gymnastics required to ponder *"What happens after we die?"* while also wondering *"What is reality, anyway?"* This kind of intelligence ventures far beyond the scope of our five major senses, exploring themes that are, as Gardner put it, *"too big or too small"* for mere perception.

Who Are the Existential Superstars?

Figure 1

When thinking of individuals with high existential intelligence, certain figures spring to mind: philosophers, religious leaders, and statespersons who can turn abstract questions into global movements or timeless art. These are the people who make grappling with metaphysical riddles look like a full-contact sport— the kind of folks who, at dinner parties, turn casual conversations into Socratic debates. But what exactly sets these existential superstars apart, and who might they be?

The Philosophical Titans

Think of Socrates, the original "why" guy, who spent his days asking tough questions that challenged conventional wisdom. His insistence on probing deeply into the meaning of justice, truth, and virtue laid the groundwork for Western philosophy. Fast-forward a couple of millennia, and you've got figures like Jean-Paul Sartre and Simone de Beauvoir, existential powerhouses who explored freedom, responsibility, and the absurdity of life. Their works, such as *Being and Nothingness* and *The Second Sex*, transformed how we think about identity, freedom, and human existence.

Religious Leaders with Profound Insight

Religious leaders often stand as paragons of existential intelligence, offering guidance on life's big questions through spiritual and philosophical lenses. The Buddha, for instance, dedicated his life to understanding the nature of suffering and how to transcend it. Similarly, figures like Jesus of Nazareth and Prophet Muhammad provided frameworks for living meaningful lives rooted in ethical principles and a sense of purpose. These leaders didn't just contemplate existential questions—they translated them into teachings that continue to shape civilizations.

Statespersons and Visionaries

In the realm of politics and leadership, existential intelligence shines in individuals who can articulate a vision that resonates on a deeply human level. Take Nelson Mandela, whose journey from political prisoner to President of South Africa exemplified resilience and a profound understanding of justice and reconciliation. Similarly, Mahatma Gandhi's philosophy of nonviolence wasn't just a political strategy; it was an existential stance on the nature of power and humanity's potential for peace.

Artists and Creatives: The Dreamers of the Human Condition

Artists with high existential intelligence translate life's mysteries into works that move us. Vincent van Gogh's *Starry Night* captures a cosmic sense of wonder and turmoil, while Franz Kafka's novels delve into the absurdities of modern existence. Poets like Rumi and Mary Oliver use words to probe love, loss, and the ineffable beauty of being alive. Even filmmakers like Ingmar Bergman and Terrence Malick weave existential themes into their narratives, asking questions that linger long after the credits roll.

The Everyday Existentialist

Not all existential superstars are historical figures or celebrities. High existential intelligence can be found in the everyday thinker— the teacher who encourages students to explore life's big questions, the caregiver who reflects on the deeper purpose of service, or the friend who always seems to ask, "What really matters to you?" These individuals may not write manifestos or create masterpieces, but their ability to engage meaningfully with existence enriches the lives of those around them.

What makes these existential superstars so compelling is their ability to confront life's ultimate questions with courage, creativity, and clarity. Whether they're crafting philosophies, inspiring movements, or creating art, these individuals remind us that grappling with the mysteries of existence isn't just a mental exercise—it's a vital part of what it means to be human. Their lives and works encourage us to think deeply, act authentically, and seek

11

meaning in our own ways. After all, in the words of Socrates, *"The unexamined life is not worth living."*

Existential Intelligence in Everyday Life

The beauty of existential intelligence is that it doesn't just show up in ivory towers or sacred texts. According to Gardner, existential musings appear in all cultures and contexts: in religion, philosophy, art, and even in gossip and bedtime stories. Think of myths and fairy tales adored by children. Beneath the dragons and magic beans, these stories often smuggle in existential themes—life, death, morality—that captivate young minds. Gardner observed that children naturally raise these profound questions, often starting with *"Why?"* and quickly escalating to *"Why, really?"* Sure, they may not always listen to the answers, but their curiosity is proof of our innate drive to make sense of existence.

A Controversial Half-Step

While Gardner's *"8½ Intelligences"* concept is as quirky as it is thought-provoking, his hesitation to grant existential intelligence full status stems from a lack of hard evidence. In his view, certain parts of the brain—perhaps the inferotemporal lobe—might be key to processing existential questions. However, Gardner also considered the possibility that such inquiries might belong to a broader *"philosophical mind"* or simply represent the most emotionally charged questions humans can ask. This scientific conservatism led Gardner to label existential intelligence as an *"8½"* rather than a full-fledged ninth intelligence, keeping it in intellectual limbo while awaiting more definitive evidence.

Existential Intelligence in Creative Expression

While existential intelligence often involves deep introspection and philosophical discussion, it also finds expression in art, music, and literature. From Dostoevsky's novels to Van Gogh's paintings, creative works that delve into existential themes resonate deeply with audiences, reflecting humanity's shared desire to find meaning and grapple with life's uncertainties. Whether through poetry, theater, or even a well-timed stand-up comedy bit, existential intelligence often manifests as an ability to translate the unanswerable into something tangible.

Why It Matters

In today's world of rapid change and existential anxiety—from climate crises to social upheaval—the capacity to ask *"Why?"* and seek purpose is more relevant than ever. Whether through personal reflection, education, or community engagement, fostering existential intelligence can help individuals navigate the chaos and find meaning in uncertainty.

In conclusion, existential intelligence may still be waiting in Gardner's *"theoretical waiting room,"* but its impact is undeniable. Whether or not it becomes the *"ninth intelligence,"* it remains a fascinating lens through which to explore the human mind and its infinite quest for understanding. So, the next time you catch yourself lost in thought, wondering about life's greatest mysteries, give yourself a little credit. You might just be flexing your existential intelligence.

Ethical Considerations in Fostering Existential Intelligence

Existential intelligence, as explored throughout this book, represents the human capacity to engage with profound questions regarding life, death, and purpose. While its cultivation offers significant benefits—enhancing critical thinking, deepening self-awareness, and fostering a sense of interconnectedness—it also introduces complex ethical considerations. The potential for misuse in leadership, education, and societal influence necessitates a careful examination of the responsibilities that accompany its development. Furthermore, fostering existential intelligence can have far-reaching implications for decision-making, social justice, and environmental stewardship. This section seeks to navigate these ethical dimensions, offering a balanced perspective on both the promise and the perils of cultivating existential intelligence.

Ethical Concerns in Leadership and Societal Influence

Leaders who possess a high degree of existential intelligence may leverage their insights to inspire and guide others. However, the ethical challenge arises when this intelligence is manipulated for personal gain or ideological control. Historical figures with profound existential insights, such as religious leaders and philosophers, have shaped societies for both good and ill.

14

- **Influence vs. Manipulation:** There is a fine line between inspiring individuals to reflect on existential questions and coercing them into specific worldviews. Ethical leadership requires transparency, respect for individual agency, and the promotion of open inquiry.

- **Ethical Decision-Making in Governance:** Existential intelligence can contribute to more reflective and morally sound policymaking. However, policies informed by existential reflections must balance philosophical depth with practical considerations, ensuring they serve diverse societal needs rather than a select few.

- **The Risk of Elitism:** Cultivating existential intelligence should not be reserved for an intellectual or socioeconomic elite. Democratizing access to philosophical education and existential exploration can prevent disparities in how this intelligence is developed and applied.

The Role of Education: Encouraging Inquiry Without Indoctrination

In educational contexts, fostering existential intelligence can encourage students to engage with profound questions, enhancing critical thinking and ethical reasoning. However, care must be taken to ensure that education remains a space for open-ended inquiry rather than ideological imposition.

- **Promoting Open-Ended Exploration:** Students should be encouraged to question and formulate their own existential beliefs rather than being directed toward predefined conclusions.

- **Diverse Perspectives:** Incorporating multiple philosophical, cultural, and religious traditions can provide students with a broad spectrum of existential perspectives, allowing them to form their own nuanced understanding.

- **Psychological Impacts:** Some existential questions—particularly those related to death, suffering, and meaning—can be distressing. Educators must create supportive environments that help students navigate existential inquiry without causing undue anxiety.

Existential Intelligence and Social Justice

Existential intelligence can play a pivotal role in fostering a just society. By encouraging individuals to reflect on ethics, purpose, and interconnectedness, this form of intelligence has the potential to drive positive social change. However, it also introduces ethical dilemmas regarding privilege, access, and practical application.

- **Empathy and Moral Responsibility:** Individuals with high existential intelligence often develop a deep sense of moral obligation. This can be leveraged to promote equity and justice, ensuring that philosophical inquiry translates into ethical action.

- **Challenges of Implementation:** While existential intelligence may encourage social responsibility, it does not automatically lead to just actions. Ethical frameworks and social structures must support the practical application of existential insights.

- **Cultural and Societal Biases:** The interpretation and application of existential intelligence may be influenced by cultural biases. A truly ethical approach must recognize and respect diverse existential perspectives.

Environmental Stewardship: An Existential Imperative

One of the most pressing ethical applications of existential intelligence lies in environmental stewardship. By fostering a deep awareness of humanity's interconnectedness with the planet, existential intelligence can serve as a catalyst for sustainable action.

- **Awareness of Future Generations:** Existential intelligence encourages individuals to consider long-term consequences, making it a valuable tool for promoting environmental responsibility.

- **Balancing Reflection and Action:** While deep existential reflection can inspire sustainable behavior, it must be coupled with concrete action. Ethical considerations arise in ensuring that existential insights lead to practical environmental initiatives.

- **The Ethical Duty to Educate:** Given the urgency of environmental crises, there is an ethical imperative to integrate existential intelligence into discussions of sustainability. However, this must be done in a way that respects diverse perspectives and lived experiences.

A Call for Ethical Stewardship

As we advance in our understanding and application of existential intelligence, ethical stewardship becomes a critical responsibility. Whether in leadership, education, social justice, or environmental action, the way existential intelligence is cultivated and applied will shape its impact on individuals and society. By fostering open inquiry, ethical responsibility, and inclusivity, we can ensure that existential intelligence serves as a force for good rather than a tool for manipulation or exclusion.

In embracing this responsibility, we uphold the true essence of existential inquiry—seeking wisdom, promoting justice, and cultivating a deeper understanding of our place in the world.

Navigating Human Depths: Exploring Existential Intelligence Across Cultures and Challenges

Between Existential Intelligence and Spiritual Intelligence

At first glance, existential intelligence and spiritual intelligence may seem like close cousins at a family reunion of human cognition—similar enough to be related, yet distinct enough to have their own personalities. However, upon closer examination, existential intelligence proves to be much broader in scope. While both transcend the traditional IQ test's "Who's the smartest in the room?" question, they each carve out unique spaces in the realm of human understanding and consciousness (Skrzypińska, 2021).

Focus and Scope: Different Lenses, Different Landscapes

Think of spiritual intelligence as the part of your mind that gazes at the stars and feels an innate connection to something greater than yourself. It involves exploring the transcendent aspects of life—accessing higher values, meaning, and purpose—while fostering a sense of harmony and compassion. Individuals with high spiritual intelligence are often guided by a desire for personal growth, interconnectedness with the world, and an inner wisdom that whispers, "There's more to life than meets the eye."

Meanwhile, existential intelligence is less concerned with "the beyond" and more focused on "the here and now." It is the ability to grapple with life's fundamental questions: Why are we here? What is the meaning of existence? What happens when we die? Those with high existential intelligence resemble the philosophers of old, endlessly curious about the mysteries of human life and the nature of reality itself.

Guidance: Who's Holding the Map?

Spiritual intelligence often follows a well-trodden path, guided by faith, spirituality, or a connection to the divine. Whether through prayer, meditation, or personal reflection, it fosters a sense of interconnectedness with the universe. This intelligence may manifest in religious practices or as a deeply personal, non-religious quest for inner peace and self-discovery.

Existential intelligence, on the other hand, does not come with a pre-drawn map. It is about confronting life's biggest questions head-on, without necessarily relying on religion or spirituality as a guide. It serves as a "DIY kit" of intelligence, encouraging individuals to contemplate mortality, freedom, and the complexities of the human condition on their own terms.

Outcomes and Applications: What Do You Get Out of It?

Those with developed spiritual intelligence often report a greater sense of inner peace, purpose, and resilience when faced with life's challenges. They tend to exhibit empathy, compassion, and a heightened ability to connect with others on their spiritual journeys. In many ways, spiritual intelligence acts as a moral compass, helping individuals navigate life's storms with wisdom and understanding.

Conversely, existential intelligence fosters authenticity and the pursuit of meaning. People with strong existential intelligence may uncover profound insights about existence, allowing them to live with greater intentionality and creativity. This type of intelligence inspires works of art, philosophical theories, and those deep, late-night conversations that leave one pondering life's mysteries.

Universality: Local vs. Global Questions

Spiritual intelligence is often tied to specific cultural and religious contexts, meaning its expression can vary widely depending on an individual's background. Spirituality in one culture may look entirely different in another, making it a beautifully diverse yet highly contextual form of intelligence.

In contrast, existential intelligence transcends cultural and religious boundaries. It deals with universal questions about human existence that people from all walks of life may contemplate at some point. Whether in a bustling city or a remote village, the questions "Why are we here?" and "What is our purpose?" remain constant.

Complex Constructs: Still a Work in Progress

Both spiritual and existential intelligence represent complex and abstract dimensions of human cognition. Researchers continue to debate their definitions, applications, and significance. While spiritual intelligence often focuses on connecting with the divine or the transcendent, existential intelligence is rooted in grappling with life's profound questions without necessarily invoking spirituality. However, both highlight the extraordinary depth of human consciousness.

In conclusion, while spiritual intelligence and existential intelligence share some overlapping terrain, they chart distinct courses through the landscape of human thought. Spiritual intelligence seeks connection and higher purpose, often through a transcendent lens, while existential intelligence delves into the heart of existence, unafraid to confront life's greatest mysteries. Whether guided by faith, philosophy, or a blend of both, these forms of intelligence remind us that the human mind is as vast and varied as the questions it seeks to answer.

Cultural Perspectives on Existential Intelligence

Existential intelligence, as conceptualized within Howard Gardner's theory of multiple intelligences, is inherently tied to the profound questions of human existence: the meaning of life, death, freedom, and purpose. While these questions are universal, the ways in which they are approached, interpreted, and answered are deeply rooted in cultural, religious, and philosophical traditions. Examining existential intelligence through a cultural lens not only enriches its conceptual framework but also underscores its practical applications in diverse educational and societal contexts. This section explores the role of culture in shaping existential intelligence, emphasizing the interplay between global traditions, individual identity, and collective worldviews.

Eastern Philosophical Traditions

Eastern philosophical traditions, particularly Buddhism, Hinduism, Daoism, and Confucianism, offer unique perspectives on existential intelligence. Although often embedded within religious frameworks, these traditions emphasize existential inquiry, self-reflection, and the pursuit of wisdom—aligning closely with Gardner's notion of existential intelligence.

Buddhism: Impermanence and Self-Transcendence

Buddhist philosophy places significant emphasis on impermanence (anicca), suffering (dukkha), and non-self (anatta) (Rahula, 1974). These concepts encourage deep existential reflection:

- *Meditation and mindfulness cultivate awareness of life's transience.*

- *The Four Noble Truths guide individuals in understanding suffering and finding meaning through enlightenment.*

- *Zen Buddhism promotes paradoxical questioning (e.g., koans) to deepen existential thought beyond rationality (Suzuki, 1956).*

Buddhism aligns existential intelligence with self-awareness, detachment from ego-driven desires, and engagement with life's uncertainties (Dalai Lama, 1999).

Hinduism: Dharma, Moksha, and the Cosmic Order

Hinduism offers profound existential insights through sacred texts like the Upanishads and the Bhagavad Gita:

- *Dharma (duty) and karma (action) frame existential intelligence within ethical decision-making and social responsibility (Eliade, 1958).*

- *Moksha (liberation from the cycle of rebirth) represents the ultimate existential realization—transcending individuality to attain unity with Brahman.*

- *The concept of Atman (self) vs. Brahman (universal consciousness) mirrors existential reflections on identity and the cosmos (Radhakrishnan & Moore, 1957).*

Through storytelling, discourse, and ritual, Hindu traditions nurture existential intelligence by encouraging reflection on fate, purpose, and interconnectedness.

Western Philosophical Traditions

Western thought has grappled with existential questions for centuries, particularly through Greek philosophy, medieval theology, and modern existentialism.

Greek Philosophy: Rational Inquiry into Existence

Ancient Greek philosophers laid the foundation for existential intelligence through critical questioning and logical reasoning (Russell, 1945).

- ***Socrates' method of inquiry (elenchus)*** *encouraged individuals to examine their beliefs, fostering self-awareness and intellectual humility (Plato, 399 BCE).*

- ***Plato's Allegory of the Cave*** *explores the journey from ignorance to enlightenment, serving as a metaphor for existential self-discovery (Plato, Republic, c. 375 BCE).*

- ***Aristotle's concept of eudaimonia*** *(flourishing) aligns with existential intelligence as a pursuit of virtue, meaning, and purpose (Aristotle, 350 BCE).*

These traditions emphasized existential inquiry as a rational, ethical, and intellectual endeavor.

Existentialism: Freedom, Absurdity, and Meaning

Modern existentialist thinkers, particularly Jean-Paul Sartre, Albert Camus, and Søren Kierkegaard, focused on individual choice, authenticity, and existential anxiety.

- ***Sartre's notion of "existence precedes essence"*** *argues that humans define their own meaning in an inherently meaningless universe (Sartre, 1982).*

- ***Camus' The Myth of Sisyphus*** *presents the human struggle against absurdity, emphasizing the importance of embracing life's lack of inherent meaning (Camus, 1942).*

- ***Kierkegaard's "leap of faith"*** *explores existential intelligence through the tension between reason, doubt, and faith (Kierkegaard, 2013).*

These perspectives illustrate how existential intelligence manifests as the ability to navigate meaninglessness, embrace freedom, and confront existential dread (Heidegger, 1988).

Indigenous and African Perspectives on Existential Intelligence

Indigenous Knowledge Systems and Existential Intelligence

Indigenous worldviews often emphasize a deep connection between human existence, nature, and the spiritual realm. In contrast to Western individualism, Indigenous perspectives view existence as relational (Battiste, 2002).

- *The concept of "seven generations" in Native American thought encourages long-term existential reflection, emphasizing responsibility to past and future generations (Cajete, 2000).*

- *Australian Aboriginal Dreamtime Stories express existential intelligence by linking ancestral wisdom, cosmology, and moral lessons through storytelling (Christie, 2008).*

- *The Andean concept of Buen Vivir promotes existential intelligence by emphasizing harmony with nature and community rather than individual self-actualization (Gudynas, 2011).*

Indigenous existential intelligence is cultivated through oral traditions, rituals, and deep ecological awareness, which contrast with Western rationalist approaches.

African Ubuntu Philosophy and Collective Existence

African existential thought is deeply rooted in community, ethics, and interdependence (Mbiti, 1969).

- *Ubuntu philosophy (Southern Africa)—"I am because we are"—emphasizes existential intelligence as a communal process rather than an individual endeavor (Ramose, 1999).*

- *Dogon cosmology (West Africa) explores existential intelligence through symbolic representations of life, death, and cosmic order (Griaule & Dieterlen, 1965).*

- *Yoruba Orunmila wisdom (Nigeria) encourages existential reflection through Ifá divination, moral reasoning, and the relationship between destiny and free will (Abimbola, 1976).*

These traditions challenge the Western emphasis on individual existential inquiry, demonstrating that meaning and purpose are often constructed collectively.

Cultural Influences on Development

Cultural backgrounds shape how existential intelligence is expressed—whether through individual introspection or communal dialogue.

Individualism vs. Collectivism in Existential Thought

Research suggests that Western societies prioritize individual existential reflection, whereas Eastern and Indigenous cultures emphasize communal existential engagement (Markus & Kitayama, 1991).

- *Western Approach* → *Focuses on personal self-actualization, aligning with existentialist thought (Maslow, 1943).*

- *Eastern Approach* → *Integrates existential intelligence within community, family, and spiritual practice (Nisbett, 2003).*

- *African Ubuntu Philosophy* → *Emphasizes "I am because we are," demonstrating a collective approach to existential reflection (Mbiti, 1969).*

These cultural variations impact how individuals confront existential dilemmas, define identity, and construct meaning.

Educational Approaches to Existential Intelligence

Different cultures embed existential exploration within their education systems:

- *Western Philosophy and Ethics Courses* → *Encourage critical thinking and debate on existential issues.*

- *Indigenous Oral Traditions* → *Teach existential wisdom through storytelling and experiential learning (Battiste, 2002).*

- ***Religious and Spiritual Education*** → *Provides structured frameworks for existential reflection within faith traditions.*

By recognizing these culturally diverse approaches, educators can develop inclusive methods to nurture existential intelligence globally.

Examining existential intelligence through a cultural perspective enriches our understanding of how societies frame, explore, and teach existential thought. While universal themes exist, cultural differences shape the expression, depth, and application of existential intelligence.

By fostering cultural inclusivity, researchers and educators can create more holistic, diverse approaches to existential learning—empowering individuals to engage with life's fundamental questions through multiple lenses.

Further Contextualization of Existential Intelligence in Modern Challenges

Existential Intelligence in the Concepts of VUCA and BANI

The concept of the VUCA world emerged in 1990, at the end of the Cold War, in response to an unpredictable landscape where American soldiers sought strategies to adapt to rapidly shifting circumstances. The acronym VUCA—representing **Volatility, Uncertainty, Complexity, and Ambiguity**—has since been widely adopted by business leaders and theorists to describe the fluid and uncertain nature of contemporary global environments (Scopi, 2023).

- *Volatility: Refers to unpredictable changes and fluctuations that affect economic, political, and social conditions, often causing significant disruptions.*

- *Uncertainty: Highlights the difficulty of predicting future events and their implications, emphasizing the lack of clarity in decision-making.*

- *Complexity: Acknowledges the intricate relationships between various factors, making it challenging to determine cause-and-effect relationships.*

- *Ambiguity: Reflects the multiple interpretations and unclear nature of information, making it difficult to discern absolute truth or meaning.*

In 2018, American anthropologist **Jamais Cascio** expanded on VUCA with the acronym **BANI—Brittle, Anxious, Nonlinear, and Incomprehensible**—to reflect the evolving complexities of the modern era. This framework gained prominence during the COVID-19 pandemic, which accelerated digital transformation and exposed vulnerabilities in social and corporate systems (Scopi, 2023).

- *Brittle: Highlights the fragility of systems that appear strong but collapse under stress.*

- *Anxious: Acknowledges the growing uncertainty and psychological impact of an unpredictable world.*

- *Nonlinear: Emphasizes the unpredictable nature of change, where small actions can lead to disproportionate consequences.*

- *Incomprehensible: Captures the overwhelming complexity of modern problems, making them difficult to fully grasp or control.*

In the face of turbulent and unpredictable environments, existential intelligence becomes a crucial tool for individuals to navigate and adapt. This form of intelligence involves the ability to reflect deeply on fundamental questions of existence, helping individuals find meaning and purpose amid uncertainty and complexity.

Fostering Meaning in Turbulence

Existential intelligence enables individuals to identify what truly matters in volatile and ambiguous situations. By focusing on core values and long-term objectives, it provides a sense of direction even in chaotic circumstances.

Building Psychological Resilience

Reflecting on existential themes such as purpose, freedom, and responsibility fosters inner strength. This helps individuals cope with stress and uncertainty by anchoring themselves to a deeper understanding of their role within a larger context.

Encouraging Adaptation and Creativity

The ability to consider multiple perspectives and explore complex questions promotes innovative thinking. Existential intelligence supports flexible problem-solving and the capacity to reframe challenges as opportunities for growth.

In a world increasingly defined by volatility, fragility, and unpredictability, existential intelligence offers a framework for navigating these challenges with clarity and purpose. Instead of panicking at life's plot twists, it helps individuals embrace uncertainty with the calm of a philosopher—or at least with fewer existential crises before breakfast. It's the art of turning chaos into opportunity, much like finding an extra fry at the bottom of the bag. By cultivating existential intelligence, individuals and organizations can build resilience and maintain a sense of purpose in an ever-changing world.

Concrete Applications of Existential Intelligence in Modern Challenges

Addressing Climate Change

Existential intelligence encourages individuals to reflect on their connection to the environment and their responsibility toward future generations. By fostering a sense of purpose and interconnectedness, this intelligence can inspire actions that prioritize sustainability. For example:

- Educational initiatives can integrate climate science with philosophical discussions on humanity's role in preserving the planet.
- Community-led projects can utilize storytelling and reflection to inspire collective environmental stewardship.

Navigating Pandemics

During crises like the COVID-19 pandemic, existential intelligence helps individuals process uncertainty and fear surrounding widespread health challenges. It provides tools for finding meaning in adversity, such as:

- Encouraging reflective practices like journaling or mindfulness to cope with anxiety and isolation.
- Promoting a sense of collective responsibility through discussions on ethical decision-making in healthcare and vaccination campaigns.

Managing Sociopolitical Instability

In times of sociopolitical unrest, existential intelligence enables individuals to critically evaluate their values and make informed decisions. This intelligence supports:

- Civic education programs that foster dialogue on justice, equality, and ethical leadership.
- Encouraging empathy and understanding in polarized societies by exploring common human values and shared existential concerns.

The Role of Education in Fostering Existential Intelligence

Education systems have a unique opportunity to cultivate existential intelligence by integrating interdisciplinary approaches that address the challenges of VUCA and BANI worlds. Practical strategies include:

- Designing curricula that combine philosophy, ethics, and social studies to explore existential questions in contemporary contexts.

- Facilitating experiential learning activities, such as community service projects, which encourage students to find meaning in their actions.

- Utilizing literature, art, and storytelling to connect students with diverse cultural perspectives on resilience and purpose.

In a world increasingly shaped by volatility, uncertainty, complexity, and ambiguity, existential intelligence serves as a vital tool for individuals to navigate modern challenges. By fostering deep reflection, critical thinking, and a search for meaning, this intelligence helps people adapt to changing circumstances while maintaining a sense of purpose.

Artificial Intelligence (AI) and Technophobia

Artificial intelligence (AI) is the superstar of computer science, capable of performing tasks that typically require human intelligence. Think machine learning, natural language processing, and computer vision—all the advanced tech that makes your smartphone smarter than you feel before your morning coffee. AI has the potential to revolutionize society, from automating mundane tasks like scheduling meetings to tackling grand challenges in medicine, transportation, and education. It's the tech equivalent of having an overachieving sibling.

But, as with any superstar, AI comes with its share of baggage. Ethical dilemmas, privacy concerns, and security risks are just the tip of the iceberg. There's also the ever-present worry about job automation, algorithmic discrimination, and the potential misuse of AI for less-than-noble purposes. And then there's the ultimate sci-fi horror story: super-intelligent AI surpassing human capabilities, sparking debates over whether we'll be the ones controlling it... or the other way around.

Enter technophobia—the irrational fear or aversion to technology. Technophobia has been around since someone probably panicked over the first wheel. When it comes to AI, this fear can lead to widespread skepticism and resistance, even when the technology has the potential to improve lives significantly. It's as if people are saying, "Sure, AI can save lives, but what if it accidentally orders 500 pizzas to my house?"

One major concern is how AI and automation might impact our sense of purpose. For many, work is closely tied to identity and societal contribution. But what happens when robots start taking over the jobs we've always done? If a machine can perform your job faster, better, and without needing coffee breaks, it's easy to feel like you're being shown the door… by a robot. This disruption can lead people to question their value in a tech-dominated job market.

As AI continues to evolve and reshape the workforce, society faces the challenge of redefining human purpose. The good news? There are still plenty of opportunities in areas that AI can't replicate (yet). Creativity, empathy, and ethics remain uniquely human strengths that robots, no matter how advanced their algorithms, cannot truly embody. Additionally, promoting lifelong learning can empower individuals to adapt to these changes, transforming career disruptions into opportunities for growth.

In this context, developing existential intelligence becomes more crucial than ever. It serves as an antidote to the nihilistic rabbit hole some might fall into when contemplating humanity's future alongside AI. Existential intelligence allows us to ask the big questions, reflect on our purpose, and embrace change with a sense of meaning and resilience. After all, while robots may excel at calculations, they'll never surpass us in contemplating the mysteries of existence—that's our domain.

Existential Neuroscience

Reference should also be made to Existential Neuroscience, an interdisciplinary field that merges concepts from neuroscience, existential philosophy, and existential psychology. It explores issues related to human existence, consciousness, and the meaning of life through a neuroscientific lens. While not yet an established discipline with a definitive knowledge base, it addresses profound questions about how neuroscience can illuminate human experiences of existence and meaning. Key areas of focus include:

Consciousness and Cognition

This area investigates how the human brain constructs and perceives reality, including self-awareness and the awareness of others. It examines how cognitive processes—such as perception, memory, and thought—shape our understanding of existence and meaning.

Emotions and Values

This branch explores how emotions and values play a crucial role in shaping our experience of existence. It examines the neural foundations of emotions and how they influence decision-making and the attribution of meaning to life.

Existential Anxiety

Existential anxiety refers to the distress stemming from awareness of one's mortality and the search for life's meaning. This field seeks to understand how such anxiety is represented in the brain and how it influences human behavior.

Free Will and Determinism

This area explores the debate between free will and determinism from a neuroscientific standpoint. Researchers investigate how decisions are made in the brain and whether choices are truly autonomous or conditioned by neural and biological processes.

Existential Psychopathology

This subfield studies how existential concerns relate to mental health conditions such as depression, anxiety, and existential spectrum disorders. It examines how neural imbalances can impact an individual's perception of meaning and purpose in life.

Existential Philosophy and Neuroscience

This area integrates concepts from existential philosophy, drawing from the works of thinkers such as Jean-Paul Sartre, Albert Camus, and Martin Heidegger. Their explorations of deep existential questions provide a foundation for neuroscientific inquiry into consciousness and human meaning-making.

It is important to note that existential neuroscience is an evolving area of research, and many of the questions it raises remain unanswered. It thrives on collaboration between scientists, philosophers, and psychologists, deepening our understanding of human experiences related to existence, consciousness, and meaning from a neuroscientific perspective.

The Experience of Existential Intelligence in Brazil: A Comparison with Conscientiology

Brazil is a country rich in philosophical, religious, and spiritual traditions, making it a fertile ground for discussions on existential intelligence. Among the various intellectual and spiritual movements in the country, Conscientiology—developed by Waldo Vieira—offers a unique perspective on human consciousness and existential questions. While existential intelligence, as conceptualized by Howard Gardner, deals with profound inquiries about meaning, existence, and purpose, Conscientiology provides a structured framework for exploring consciousness, past lives, and multidimensionality.

This chapter examines the Brazilian experience with existential intelligence, comparing it with the principles of Conscientiology and analyzing Waldo Vieira's own existential insights.

Existential Intelligence in Brazil: A Cultural Perspective

Brazil's diverse cultural landscape plays a significant role in shaping its engagement with existential questions. From Indigenous traditions and Afro-Brazilian religions like Candomblé and Umbanda to the widespread influence of Catholicism and Spiritism, Brazilians have historically sought answers to profound existential inquiries.

Unlike many Western societies that approach existential questions primarily through philosophy or secular thought, Brazil deeply integrates spirituality into its cultural fabric. This is evident in educational institutions, religious communities, and even everyday conversations, where discussions on the meaning of life, reincarnation, and spiritual evolution are common. The Brazilian perspective on existential intelligence tends to be holistic, blending science, philosophy, and spirituality—an approach that closely aligns with Conscientiology's framework.

After all, in Brazil, questioning the meaning of life is just another Saturday afternoon activity—right before churrasco and samba.

Waldo Vieira's Existential Intelligence: Thinking Beyond the Physical Body

Figure 2 - Waldo Vieira in Holociclo (Ceaec)

Source: http://100fronteiras.com/

Figure 3 - Centro de Altos Estudos da Conscienciologia – Ceaec

(Source: https://campusceaec.org/aleia-dos-genios/)

If existential intelligence is about pondering life's greatest questions, Waldo Vieira could be considered one of Brazil's foremost existential thinkers—except he didn't stop at just asking questions. He went a step further, creating an entire discipline dedicated to exploring consciousness beyond the material world.

Vieira's existential intelligence wasn't about debating whether the glass is half full or half empty. He likely would have asked, *"Which dimension is this glass from, and did my consciousness choose to incarnate in this reality just to drink from it?"* His intellectual curiosity led him to transition from Spiritism—having worked closely with Chico Xavier, Brazil's most famous medium— to developing Conscientiology, a systematic study of consciousness that includes concepts such as extraphysical projections, bioenergies, and multidimensional evolution.

Waldo Vieira's approach to existential intelligence was highly experimental. While traditional existential philosophers like Sartre and Camus wrote about the absurdity of existence, Vieira was busy conducting out-of-body experiments to explore what existence looked like beyond the physical realm. Who needs existential dread when you can have an astral projection?

Conscientiology and Existential Intelligence: Points of Convergence and Divergence

What Is Conscientiology?

Conscientiology, founded by Waldo Vieira, is a Brazilian philosophical-scientific movement that studies consciousness beyond the physical body. Unlike traditional psychology or neuroscience, which focus on cognition and behavior, Conscientiology explores multidimensionality, bioenergies, out-of-body experiences, and the concept of *intermissive courses*—pre-life planning of reincarnation.

Within Conscientiology, Vieira introduced *Projectiology*, a discipline that investigates out-of-body experiences (OBEs) and other parapsychic phenomena. He argued that human consciousness is not confined to the physical body and that experiences such as lucid projections provide insight into a broader existential reality.

Similarities Between Existential Intelligence and Conscientiology

1. **Deep Reflection on Existence** – Both frameworks encourage individuals to question the meaning of life, the nature of existence, and their purpose within a larger reality.

2. **Self-Knowledge and Personal Development** – Existential intelligence emphasizes introspection, while Conscientiology promotes self-research as a means of better understanding one's consciousness.

3. **Ethical and Moral Reasoning** – Both perspectives recognize the importance of ethics in existential exploration, whether through Gardner's intelligence framework or Vieira's *cosmoethics* (universal ethics based on multidimensional reality).

4. **Integration of Science and Spirituality** – Existential intelligence explores life's big questions without necessarily relying on religion, while Conscientiology attempts to study spiritual and existential phenomena through a scientific paradigm.

Key Differences

1. **Multidimensionality vs. Philosophical Reflection** – Existential intelligence remains within cognitive and philosophical domains, whereas Conscientiology actively studies multidimensional experiences, reincarnation, and extraphysical consciousness.

2. **Empirical Validation** – Existential intelligence, despite its challenges, aims to be measurable within the framework of cognitive psychology, while Conscientiology relies on personal experience and subjective exploration, making scientific validation difficult.

3. **Purpose of Inquiry** – Existential intelligence seeks to understand *why* we exist, while Conscientiology also

explores *how* consciousness evolves across multiple lifetimes and dimensions.

4. **Education and Dissemination** – Conscientiology has formal institutions that offer structured courses, whereas existential intelligence remains a theoretical concept applied in education and psychology without a dedicated institutional framework.

Although existential intelligence and Conscientiology differ in methodology and epistemology, both perspectives contribute to the ongoing quest for meaning and self-awareness in Brazilian society. Whether through deep philosophical contemplation or direct experimentation with multidimensional consciousness, these frameworks invite individuals to explore the ultimate questions of existence in their own way.

Building the Foundations: Theoretical Insights into Existential Intelligence

This chapter outlines the foundational theories and concepts that support the study, providing a critical review of recent literature from 2018 to 2023. By synthesizing current research, it offers a comprehensive contextualization of existential intelligence and its intersections with education, psychology, and broader societal trends.

Digital Games in Educational Contexts and Multiple Intelligences: Approaches and Contributions to Learning

Digital games have increasingly been utilized as educational tools due to their potential to engage students in an active and meaningful way. In academic settings, they can be designed to address specific curriculum topics, creating a playful and motivating learning environment.

Ramos and Martins (2018) explored the integration of digital screens and new technologies in educational contexts, which require various skills and engage multiple intelligences. Their study aimed to identify how digital games exercise different forms of intelligence in educational settings. To achieve this, they conducted exploratory research with a quantitative approach, administering a questionnaire to 58 students enrolled in the Extension Course in Continuing Education in School Councils. The objective was to evaluate the students' experience using an educational game as part of their coursework.

Regarding existential intelligence, students were asked whether they perceived ethical and moral issues while playing the game, as a means of assessing this particular domain of intelligence. The results revealed that logical-mathematical intelligence was the most utilized, followed by existential intelligence, abstraction, spatial intelligence, and motor coordination. The authors concluded that recognizing the engagement of multiple intelligences in digital game interactions reinforces the educational potential of such tools and highlights their diverse pedagogical applications.

The intersection between digital games and the theory of Multiple Intelligences presents a promising approach to enhancing learning. Digital games can be designed to stimulate various types of intelligence, providing challenges that involve a broad range of cognitive and practical skills. This multidimensional approach has the potential to accommodate students' diverse learning needs, fostering more comprehensive and holistic education.

Existential Intelligence Among Students at World Islamic Sciences University in Jordan

Al Jaddou (2018) conducted a study investigating existential intelligence among students at World Islamic Sciences University in Jordan. The primary objective was to assess the degree of existential intelligence among participants and to examine possible influences of variables such as gender, field of study, experience, marital status, and professional position. The study sampled 56 students from the Faculty of Educational Sciences, utilizing the Existential Intelligence Scale adapted by Zubi et al. (2015).

The results indicated that the participants exhibited an average degree of existential intelligence. Additionally, no statistically significant differences were found based on gender, specialization, experience, marital status, or professional position. These findings suggest that, in the educational context analyzed, existential intelligence is not strongly influenced by these demographic and experiential variables.

Differences in Multiple Intelligences Among Students at Jordan University of Science and Technology

Ayasrah and Aljarrah (2020) conducted a study examining variations in multiple intelligences among students at Jordan University of Science and Technology, focusing on factors such as gender, academic year, and performance. The research sample included 349 students of both sexes. The methodology employed descriptive analysis, using the MacKenzie scale for multiple intelligences, which assessed nine dimensions, each represented by ten items.

The findings revealed no statistically significant differences related to gender or academic year. However, significant differences were observed in several dimensions when analyzed in relation to academic performance—except in the musical and existential intelligence domains. The study contributed to increasing students' self-awareness regarding their intellectual strengths while also offering insights for developing academic programs aimed at improving performance. These results highlight the complexity of the relationship between multiple intelligences and academic success, suggesting that different intelligences may influence students' achievements in distinct ways.

The Resurgence of Interest in Existential Intelligence: Why Now?

Twelve years after introducing the theory of Multiple Intelligences (1983), Howard Gardner speculated about the possibility of a ninth intelligence—*existential intelligence*. He described it as the cognitive ability to raise and ponder profound, philosophical questions—questions about love, morality, life, and death—in essence, about the nature and quality of existence. Gardner noted that nearly all children ask these types of questions, though most young people are more focused on asking them rather than deeply contemplating potential answers. He suggested that existential inquiry is primarily the domain of philosophers and religious leaders, though most individuals engage in such reflection periodically, particularly when confronted with art and literature.

At the time, Gardner hesitated to classify existential intelligence as a fully distinct intelligence, as he was uncertain whether it met the criteria he had established for independent intelligences. Specifically, he questioned whether it had a neurological or biological basis, whether it was a universal cognitive capacity or one that emerged primarily in post-Socratic societies, and whether it was truly a separate intelligence or merely an amalgamation of already recognized intelligences—such as linguistic, logical-mathematical, and intrapersonal intelligences. Moreover, he insisted that existential intelligence should not be conflated with religious, spiritual, or sacred capacities.

Gardner (2020) revisited the concept of existential intelligence, noting a resurgence of interest, particularly during the COVID-19 pandemic. He observed a significant increase in inquiries related to this domain, likely influenced by the unprecedented challenges and uncertainties brought about by the global crisis. The pandemic created conditions in which many individuals had more time for self-reflection, leading to heightened engagement with existential questions. Issues surrounding life, death, human vulnerability, and purpose became more prominent, reinforcing the relevance of existential intelligence in contemporary discourse.

He claimed that some scholars were eager to determine whether existential intelligence met the necessary criteria to be officially recognized as an intelligence. However, he responded that it had not yet reached that status and remained in a state of limbo. Some researchers sought a formal test to assess this intelligence, while others asserted that they had already developed one. Gardner (2020) clarified that he had not created any such tests but expressed his willingness to provide feedback to those who submitted sample assessments.

Regarding the assumption by certain writers that existential intelligence had already been established as a legitimate phenomenon—and that it was synonymous with "spiritual" or "religious" intelligence—Gardner argued otherwise. He maintained that *existential intelligence* involves raising and contemplating profound questions, which *may or may not* include spiritual or religious themes. For instance, pondering the vastness of the universe or reflecting on the significance of a single grain of sand would also fall within its domain.

A Valid Evaluation of the Theory of Multiple Intelligences: Methodological Quality Problems in Intervention Studies

In a study conducted by Ferrero, Vadillo, and Léon (2021), researchers aimed to assess the impact of interventions related to Multiple Intelligences on academic performance. These interventions sought to apply the theory in educational contexts to enhance student learning and development. To evaluate their effectiveness, the researchers analyzed studies that quantitatively measured the impact of Multiple Intelligence-based interventions on academic performance using a pre-post design with a control group.

The systematic review included 39 English-language studies involving 3,009 students from preschool to high school across 14 different countries. However, the analysis revealed significant methodological flaws in the reviewed studies. Among the most notable issues were small sample sizes and the absence of active control groups. Additionally, many studies lacked detailed information about the measurement tools used and the specific activities conducted during the interventions.

The authors concluded that a valid evaluation of Multiple Intelligence-based interventions remains impossible due to these methodological shortcomings. The absence of robust data on measurement tools, intervention activities, and potential publication bias has hindered a clear understanding of the effectiveness of Multiple Intelligence-inspired methodologies in educational settings. Consequently, as of that time, empirical evidence supporting the distinct existence of Multiple Intelligences remained weak.

Consumerism Versus the Culture of Existential Intelligence

Modern society is characterized by the dominance of consumerism, where the acquisition of goods, services, and experiences becomes a central focus of people's lives. Consumerism is fueled by advertising, media influence, and societal pressures that promote the notion that happiness and success are attainable through material consumption. However, this pursuit often leads to a superficial sense of fulfillment, where the continuous acquisition of possessions replaces the deeper search for meaning and purpose.

Existential intelligence, as introduced by Gardner (1983), encompasses the ability to explore profound questions about existence, meaning, and life's purpose. It involves philosophical and existential inquiry that extends beyond the immediate gratification associated with consumerism. The quest for meaning is an intrinsic aspect of human experience, as individuals seek to understand their place in the world and cultivate a deeper sense of purpose.

A study by Elena Nedelcu (2021) examined the challenges individuals face in finding existential meaning within a consumer-driven society. The author argued that consumerism often fosters an illusion of self-sufficiency and fulfillment, where the pursuit of material wealth is mistaken for a genuine search for purpose. However, this superficial pursuit frequently leaves little room for profound existential reflection, ultimately leading to a disconnection from deeper aspects of life.

The study raises the question of whether consumerism serves as a genuine barrier to the development of existential intelligence. Additionally, the author explores the idea that fostering awareness of existential intelligence may provide a solution to the dilemmas posed by consumerism. By prioritizing the search for meaning and purpose, society may counterbalance the negative effects of rampant consumerism and redirect its focus toward deeper and more meaningful pursuits.

The Existential Intelligence Scale and Its Implications for the Preliminary Assessment of Ontological Insecurity

Fernandes (2021) proposed the Existential Intelligence Scale (EIS), an instrument designed to measure an individual's ability to engage in introspection regarding fundamental existential elements such as death, origins, and the nature of reality. The EIS, consisting of 12 items, was developed in response to the author's dissatisfaction with previous existential scales, which, in her view, failed to adequately capture the complexity of existential exploration. The creation of the EIS reflected a commitment to assessing existential intelligence with greater depth and precision.

The study also addressed the debate over incorporating spirituality into the assessment of existential intelligence. The author argued that while spirituality is a significant aspect of human experience, its inclusion in the existential intelligence scale presents challenges. Previous scales struggled to integrate spiritual elements effectively, as spirituality often involves supernatural beliefs and religious perspectives. The author cited Gardner (2000), who shared similar concerns, emphasizing the lack of empirical evidence supporting supernatural phenomena and highlighting the need to distinguish between personal beliefs and the phenomenological aspects of spirituality.

The EIS demonstrated internal consistency and established significant correlations with depression and stress, though not with anxiety. These findings suggest a connection between existential exploration and certain aspects of psychological well-being, underscoring the relevance of existential intelligence in mental health discussions. However, the study acknowledged its limitations and emphasized the need for future research to further explore the relationship between existential intelligence, spirituality, and other psychological constructs.

Pro-environmental Behavior and Existential Intelligence

Pro-environmental behavior refers to individual actions that demonstrate concern for the environment and a commitment to its preservation and sustainability.

The Adiwiyata program is an initiative of the Ministry of Environment in Indonesia that aims to promote environmental awareness and conservation among students. Adiwiyata schools adopt ecologically sustainable practices and educate students on the importance of environmental preservation from an early age. The program seeks to empower students to become active environmental advocates and agents of change in their communities.

A study conducted by Susana Adi Astuti, Andreas Lako, and Margaretha Sih Setija Utami (2021) examined the relationship between existential intelligence and pro-environmental behavior among students from both Adiwiyata and non-Adiwiyata schools. A total of 1,539 high school students from Semarang participated in the study between April and June 2021. Data were analyzed using the non-parametric statistical method of Mann-Whitney. The idea that existential intelligence may be linked to environmental awareness and pro-environmental behavior is intriguing, as existential exploration can foster a deeper appreciation of the interconnection between individuals and their environment.

The study introduced a new perspective on predicting pro-environmental behavior through existential intelligence. The hypothesis suggested that students with higher existential intelligence may be more inclined to adopt behaviors that promote environmental conservation. This is because existential exploration can lead to heightened sensitivity to environmental issues and a deeper understanding of the individual's role in maintaining the ecosystem.

The survey results indicated that students from Adiwiyata schools demonstrated higher levels of both existential intelligence and pro-environmental behavior compared to students from non-Adiwiyata schools. This finding suggests a possible connection between the Adiwiyata program's educational approach—emphasizing environmental awareness—and the development of students' existential intelligence.

Existential Intelligence Among University Students: The Influence of Gender and Level of Study

A study by Anshuman Sharma and Arbind Kumar Jha (2021) focused on assessing existential intelligence among university and non-university students, exploring variations based on gender and level of study. The gender analysis aimed to determine whether men and women exhibit statistically significant differences in their capacity for existential thinking. Similarly, the study investigated whether students at different academic levels—postgraduate, graduate, and non-graduate—show significant variations in existential intelligence.

To achieve these objectives, the researchers used the Existential Thinking Capacity Scale (ETAS) as an assessment instrument in a sample of 102 students. The findings revealed no statistically significant differences in existential intelligence between students based on gender or academic level. In other words, there was no evidence to suggest that men and women, or students at varying educational stages, displayed meaningful differences in their ability to engage with existential questions.

Existential Intelligence and the Adversity Quotient: Fostering Intelligent Learners

In contexts of adversity—such as the COVID-19 pandemic—the capabilities inherent in existential intelligence can play a crucial role in individuals' adaptation and resilience when facing complex challenges. The pandemic brought widespread disruptions, affecting not only physical health but also mental, emotional, social, and spiritual well-being. The loss of lives and jobs, along with the disruption of daily routines, created an environment of adversity that demanded a holistic approach to coping.

In their 2022 study, Paramasivam et al. explored existential intelligence as a form of spiritual adaptation in times of crisis. The authors proposed that existential intelligence could help individuals find meaning and self-actualization amid hardship, encouraging them to appreciate life's moments through spiritual and religious perspectives.

The study examined the relationship between existential intelligence and the adversity quotient (AQ). The authors identified connections between intelligence quotient (IQ), emotional quotient

(EQ), and spiritual quotient (SQ), suggesting that intrapersonal competencies related to existential intelligence contribute to individuals' ability to navigate adversity effectively.

The researchers argued that exploring existential intelligence and its applications could promote self-fulfillment and well-being, even during crises like the COVID-19 pandemic. Deepening our understanding of how existential intelligence influences AQ is essential for recognizing how spiritual and existential aspects can enhance resilience in challenging situations.

Who Are We as Humans? A Question Raised by Existential Intelligence

The quest to understand one's identity and existence has been a central theme throughout history. Questions about humanity's place in the universe and the essence of human existence have been explored in various cultures, philosophies, and traditions. The ongoing search for answers to fundamental questions—such as *Who are we?* and *What is our purpose?*—reflects humanity's innate desire to comprehend the core of existence.

An article by Anshuman Sharma and Arbind Kumar Jha (2022) examined the intrinsic nature of existential intelligence and its role in provoking deep reflection on existential questions. Existential intelligence is characterized by its ability to encourage individuals to contemplate aspects of life that transcend everyday sensory experiences, prompting them to explore profound, multifaceted questions without simple answers.

Discovering Existential Intelligence

The authors highlighted the unique nature of existential intelligence, arguing that it cannot be confined to rigid definitions. Instead, they described it as a concept that connects individuals to epistemological and metaphysical realities. Existential intelligence fosters contemplation of both vast and subtle existential questions, as demonstrated by historical figures and thinkers such as Buddha, Sartre, Sagan, and Frankl, who profoundly explored human existence and its meaning.

The study further examined various theoretical perspectives on existential intelligence. Gardner (1999) proposed it as a biopsychological potential, while Jaddou (2018) conceptualized it as a multidimensional modality. Meanwhile, Neisser et al. (1996) approached existential intelligence as an information-processing agent, whereas Bühner et al. (2008) and Stadler et al. (2015) considered it a problem-solving skill.

The article emphasized that existential intelligence could enable individuals to live authentically, imbuing seemingly meaningless situations with purpose. This capacity for deep reflection and introspection allows people to confront existential challenges and crises with a more profound, informed perspective. Through existential intelligence, individuals can transcend the pursuit of immediate answers and explore the deeper and more nuanced dimensions of existence.

Flávia Ceccato

On the Experience of Meaning at Work and in Organizations: Contributions of Logotherapy and Existential Analysis

The relationship between individuals and their work has been a crucial issue in contemporary society, as a significant portion of human life is dedicated to professional activities. The investment of time, energy, and dedication in the workplace is substantial, leading to increasing expectations regarding professional fulfillment. Given this importance, the article *"On the Experience of Meaning at Work and in Organizations: Contributions of Logotherapy and Existential Analysis"* by Rafael Rebouças Andrade, Márcia Fernanda Moreno dos Santos Ferreira, and Rickardo Léo Ramos Gomes (2023) provides a comprehensive exploration of how Logotherapy and Existential Analysis contribute to the understanding of work and organizational life.

At the heart of the article is the centrality of meaning in life, as emphasized by Logotherapy and Existential Analysis. These approaches highlight how individuals understand and attribute significance to their actions, relationships, and interactions in professional settings. Logotherapy, developed by Viktor Frankl, and Existential Analysis offer a conceptual framework for exploring human experiences in the workplace.

The researchers employed a qualitative approach through a narrative review to examine the connections between the fundamental principles of Logotherapy and Existential Analysis and their relevance to modern work environments. This methodology enabled an in-depth analysis of how these concepts shape the experience of work and organizational culture.

The study's findings underscored the profound impact of Existential Analytical thought when applied to the meaning of work and organizational settings. A key conclusion was the necessity of fostering more humane workplaces—ones that acknowledge and value the existential dimension of employees, thereby enhancing workplace fulfillment and meaning.

This research contributes to a reassessment of the relationship between meaning and work in contemporary society, encouraging deeper reflection on the interactions between individuals and organizations. Through the lens of Logotherapy and Existential Analysis, the authors advocate for greater contemplation of purpose and significance in work-related activities, promoting a more holistic and human-centered view of professional life.

Existential Nihilism Scale (ENS): Theory, Development, and Psychometric Assessment

Existential nihilism—the belief that existence lacks inherent meaning and that efforts to ascribe meaning are ultimately futile—is a complex philosophical perspective that has influenced cultural and intellectual history. However, its impact on mental health and broader society has remained underexplored due to the absence of a scientific framework for measurement. The article *"The Existential Nihilism Scale (ENS): Theory, Development, and Psychometric Evaluation"* by Jeremy Forsythe and Myriam Mongrain (2023) seeks to bridge this gap by introducing the Existential Nihilism Scale (ENS), a tool designed to quantify this philosophical construct.

The authors defined existential nihilism as a worldview that asserts the absence of meaning in life while rejecting any attempt to impose meaning upon existence. The historical trajectory of nihilism in philosophy and culture is complex and often ambiguous. Despite its intellectual influence, its effects on mental health and societal well-being have remained relatively unexamined due to the lack of a standardized assessment tool.

To address this limitation, the authors developed the Existential Nihilism Scale (ENS), an eight-item instrument meticulously designed to measure the construct with precision. The scale was created following rigorous psychometric and theoretical guidelines to ensure its validity and reliability.

To evaluate the ENS, the authors conducted two parallel studies one with a sample of university students and another with a community-based group. These studies assessed various aspects of the scale, including item quality, internal structure, and multiple forms of validity, such as convergent, concurrent, discriminant, and incremental validity. The findings demonstrated that the ENS possesses robust psychometric properties, confirming its effectiveness as a reliable tool for assessing existential nihilism.

The ENS emerges as a promising instrument for future research exploring the impact of existential nihilism on mental health, well-being, and societal outcomes. Its introduction significantly advances the scientific understanding and measurement of this complex philosophical stance, offering valuable insights into how nihilistic perspectives shape human experiences.

Existential nihilism stands in direct contrast to the concept of existential intelligence. However, insights from the development of the ENS could prove valuable in constructing a scale to evaluate existential intelligence as a domain within Multiple Intelligences theory.

Methodological Approach to Assessing Existential Intelligence

The methodological framework for this study builds on established principles for identifying and validating intelligences, as outlined by Gardner (1983) and refined by Kornhaber, Fierros, and Veneema (2004). By applying these criteria to existential intelligence, the methodology seeks to assess the extent to which this proposed domain aligns with the broader theory of multiple intelligences. The following steps outline the comprehensive approach adopted in this investigation:

Step 1: Applying Gardner's Criteria to Existential Intelligence

Gardner's criteria for identifying an intelligence include neurological evidence, core operations, evolutionary history, developmental trajectories, and symbolic representation, among others. The application of these criteria to existential intelligence involves the following processes:

- **Neurological Basis**: Reviewing neuropsychological studies to identify brain regions potentially linked to existential thought, such as the prefrontal cortex or areas associated with abstract reasoning and introspection.

- **Core Operations**: Analyzing the ability to engage with existential questions—such as the meaning of life, mortality, and purpose—as fundamental cognitive processes.

- **Cultural and Historical Evidence**: Examining how existential themes have consistently emerged across cultures and historical periods, emphasizing their universality and significance in human development.

- **Developmental Trajectory**: Investigating whether existential intelligence manifests early in childhood, as Gardner suggests for established intelligences, and how it evolves throughout an individual's lifespan.

- **Symbolic Representation**: Exploring how existential concepts are expressed through literature, art, philosophy, and religious traditions, demonstrating their integration into human symbolic systems.

Step 2: Defining Characteristics of High Existential Intelligence

Individuals with high levels of existential intelligence exhibit distinct traits, including:

- **Reflective Thinking**: A strong tendency to deeply contemplate abstract and philosophical questions.

- **Sensitivity to Purpose and Meaning**: An inclination to seek meaning in life experiences and a heightened awareness of their existential significance.

- **Ethical and Moral Reasoning**: The ability to consider ethical dilemmas and questions of justice, often reflecting on the broader implications of their choices.

- **Interconnected Perspective**: A capacity to perceive connections between oneself, others, and the universe, fostering empathy and a sense of shared existence.

This step synthesizes findings from existing literature and case studies to establish a profile of individuals with heightened existential intelligence.

Step 3: Analysis of Existing Psychometric Questionnaires

Since existential intelligence involves complex and abstract aspects of human cognition, designing an accurate test to measure it remains challenging. Traditional intelligence tests assess quantifiable skills, whereas existential intelligence is rooted in deep reflection on life's meaning. This step examines existing scales and their limitations, including:

- **The Scale for Existential Thinking** (Allan & Shearer, 2012)

- **The Adapted Scale for Existential Thinking** (Zubi et al., 2015)

- **The Existential Intelligence Scale** (Fernandes, 2021)

- **The Multiple Intelligence Inventory** (McKenzie, 1999)

A comparative analysis highlights the strengths and limitations of each scale. To enhance neutrality, religious terminology should be reworded in more philosophical or existential terms, ensuring broad applicability across diverse belief systems.

Step 4: Proposal of Psychometric Questionnaires

Two new psychometric instruments are introduced, tailored to different age groups:

- **Questionnaire for Adolescents and Adults (20 Items)**:

  This instrument comprehensively evaluates existential intelligence, focusing on domains such as ethical reasoning, purpose-seeking, and reflective thinking. The 20 items incorporate scenarios and prompts that encourage respondents to articulate their thought processes.

- **Questionnaire for Children (5 Items)**:

Recognizing the developmental stage of younger individuals, this shorter questionnaire simplifies existential themes into accessible questions, such as exploring their thoughts on purpose or their relationship with nature and others.

Both tools are structured to facilitate future validation studies, ensuring they meet rigorous psychometric standards and are adaptable across cultural contexts.

This methodological approach provides a systematic and comprehensive framework for advancing the study of existential intelligence. By applying Gardner's criteria, defining core characteristics, critically analyzing existing tools, and proposing new psychometric instruments, this study lays the foundation for further empirical validation and practical applications. Ultimately, this methodology bridges theoretical insights with actionable tools, enhancing our understanding of existential intelligence and its relevance in diverse educational and societal settings.

Flávia Ceccato

Examining the Criteria for Existential Intelligence and Its Implications

Criteria for Identifying an Intelligence

As mentioned earlier, Howard Gardner's theory of multiple intelligences introduced the idea of existential intelligence, which, let's be honest, sounds like the kind of intelligence you develop after a long shower thought or a deep conversation at 2 a.m. Unlike well-established intelligences such as logical-mathematical or linguistic intelligence, existential intelligence remains in the academic waiting room, seeking greater recognition. Since it's not as clearly defined as its more popular counterparts, it's crucial to describe it as thoroughly as possible while closely adhering to Gardner's guidelines.

Gardner (1983) and Kornhaber, Fierros, & Veneema (2004) established eight criteria for identifying an intelligence as distinct, as outlined in the following table:

Table 1. Criteria for Identifying an Intelligence

Criteria for Identifying an Intelligence
1. It should be observed in relative isolation among prodigies, individuals with autism, stroke victims, or other exceptional populations. In other words, certain individuals must exhibit exceptionally high or low levels of a particular ability compared to other cognitive capacities.
2. It must have a distinct neural representation—meaning its neural structure and functioning should be distinguishable from other major human faculties.
3. It must follow a unique developmental trajectory, with different intelligences developing at varying rates and along separate paths.
4. It must have a basis in evolutionary biology. In other words, an intelligence should have a prior presence in primates or other species and demonstrate potential survival value.
5. It must be capable of being represented through symbol systems, such as those used in formal or informal education..
6. It should be supported by evidence from psychometric intelligence tests.
7. It must be distinguishable from other intelligences through experimental psychological tasks.
8. It must demonstrate a central information-processing system, meaning there must be identifiable mental processes that specifically handle information related to this intelligence..

Source: Gardner (1983); Kornhaber, Fierros, & Veneema (2004).

Analyzing Each Criterion in Relation to Existential Intelligence

Personalities with a High Level of Existential Intelligence

"It should be seen in relative isolation in prodigies, individuals with autism, stroke victims, or other exceptional populations. In other words, certain individuals must demonstrate particularly high or low levels of a particular ability in contrast to other capacities."

It is not surprising that many of history's most influential figures can be considered to have possessed high existential intelligence. Renowned philosophers such as Plato, Aristotle, Immanuel Kant, and Friedrich Nietzsche, along with contemporary thinkers like Stephen Hawking and Richard Dawkins, have extensively explored topics related to existential intelligence. From a scientific perspective, this intelligence is evident in studies on the origins of the universe, consciousness, and the mysteries of reality.

The great existential questions—those concerning human existence, reality, and meaning—have been subjects of profound reflection and debate throughout history. Below are some of the major existential questions and the thinkers who have contributed to them:

- **The meaning of life and the purpose of existence:**
  - Austrian psychiatrist Viktor Frankl explored the search for meaning and purpose in his book *Man's Search for Meaning.*

- **The nature of reality and existence:**

  o German philosopher Martin Heidegger examined human existence and the nature of reality in *Being and Time.*

  o French philosopher Jean-Paul Sartre addressed themes of freedom, responsibility, and the human condition in *Being and Nothingness.*

- **The relationship between humanity and the divine:**

  o Medieval theologian and philosopher St. Thomas Aquinas explored faith, reason, and the existence of God in *Summa Theologica.*

  o Danish philosopher Søren Kierkegaard tackled faith, anxiety, and individual existence in works such as *The Sickness Unto Death* and *Fear and Trembling.*

- **The issue of mortality and the search for meaning:**

  o French philosopher Albert Camus discussed the absurdity of life and the struggle for meaning in *The Stranger* and *The Myth of Sisyphus.*

- **The pursuit of happiness and personal fulfillment:**

  o Greek philosopher Epicurus proposed a philosophy centered on the pursuit of happiness and personal satisfaction, known as *Epicureanism.*

- **The relationship between mind and body, and the nature of consciousness:**

    o French philosopher and mathematician René Descartes explored the mind-body relationship and the nature of consciousness in his famous statement: *"Cogito, ergo sum"* (I think, therefore I am).

Religious Figures and Existential Intelligence

Prominent religious leaders throughout history have also demonstrated high existential intelligence. Some notable examples include:

- **Buddha:** The founder of Buddhism, his name literally means *"one who is awake."* Born in Nepal, he taught in India between the sixth and fourth centuries B.C., emphasizing the pursuit of higher truths.

- **Jesus Christ:** As the central figure of Christianity, Jesus challenged the status quo of first-century Jerusalem, presenting a belief in a higher being—God—who embodies eternal truth.

- **St. Augustine:** An early Christian theologian, St. Augustine drew heavily from Plato's philosophy, advocating that life should be spent searching for higher abstract truths beyond the imperfections of the physical world.

The following table further highlights additional individuals recognized for their high level of existential intelligence.

Table 2: Personalities with a High Level of Existential Intelligence

Personalities	Contributions	Connection with Ex I
Socrates	Greek philosopher, Socratic method	Ask deeper and deeper questions for the understanding of the truth
Plato	Greek philosopher, abstract truth	The highest and most complete truth we witness in real life
Friedrich Nietzsche	German philosopher and philologist	Precursor of the existentialist movement
Karl Jasper	German philosopher	Man's direct concern for his own existence
Simone de Beauvoir	French writer	Relates phenomenological-existential arguments
Wayne Dyer	American author and speaker	Spiritual aspects of human experience and potential to live an extraordinary life

Source: Paramasivam et al, 2022 (adapted).

Given the above, it is evident that existential intelligence can be observed in relative isolation among prodigies and other exceptional individuals. The figures mentioned in this section demonstrated significantly high levels of existential intelligence compared to the general population, achieving remarkable prominence in their respective eras.

Neural Structure and Functioning

"It must have a distinct neural representation—that is, its neural structure and functioning must be distinguishable from that of other major human faculties."

Neural structure refers to the organization and arrangement of nerve cells, or neurons, within the nervous system. The nervous system consists of billions of neurons that connect to form complex circuits and communication networks, enabling information processing and control over various bodily functions. Neural structure describes how these nerve cells are organized and how they interact with one another.

The neural structure is highly specialized and varies across different parts of the nervous system, including the brain, spinal cord, and peripheral nerves. Key features of neural structure include:

- **Neurons**: The fundamental units of the nervous system, neurons are specialized cells responsible for transmitting electrical and chemical signals. They consist of dendrites (which receive signals), a cell body (where processing occurs), and an axon (which transmits signals to other cells) (Santos, 2002).

- **Synapses**: These are the connections between neurons. At synapses, neurons communicate by releasing neurotransmitters, which influence the electrical activity of neighboring cells (Santos, 2002).

- **Neural Circuits**: These are specific patterns of neural connections dedicated to particular functions. For example, neural circuits regulate vision, movement, language, and various cognitive and motor abilities (Tafner, 1998).

- **Brain Areas**: The brain's neural structure is divided into distinct regions, each responsible for specific functions. For instance, the frontal cortex is associated with planning and motor control, while the temporal cortex plays a crucial role in auditory processing and language comprehension (Santos, 2002).

Figure 4. Specialized functions of the cortex

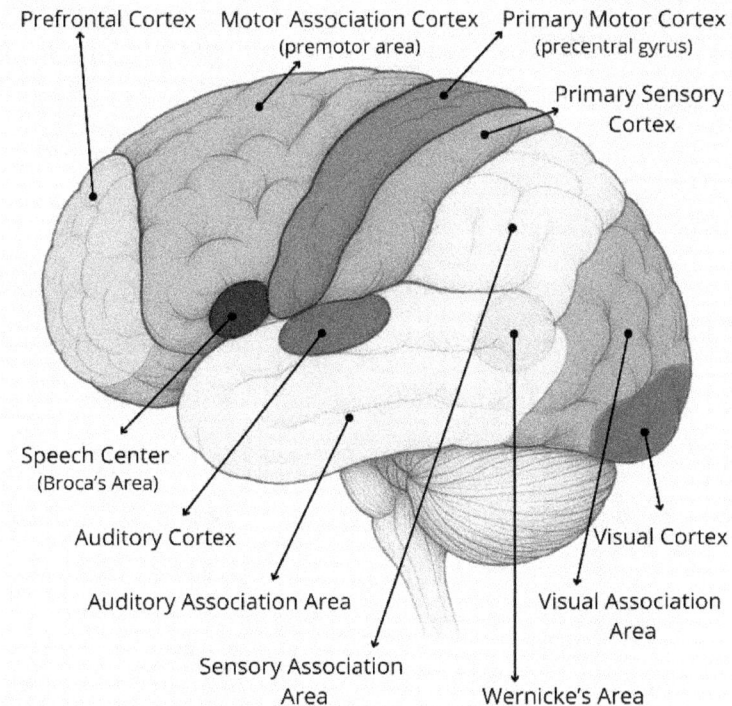

Cortical Area	Function
Prefrontal Cortex	Planning, emotion, judgment
Motor Association Cortex (premotor area)	Coordination of complex movements
Primary Motor Cortex (precentral gyrus)	Initiation of motor behavior
Primary Sensory Cortex	Receives tactile information from the body (touch, vibration, temperature, pain)
Sensory Association Area	Multisensory information processing
Visual Association Area	Complex visual information processing
Visual Cortex	Simple visual stimulus detection
Speech Center (Broca's Area)	Speech production and articulation
Auditory Cortex	Sound intensity detection
Auditory Association Area	Complex auditory information processing and memory
Wernicke's Area	Language comprehension

Source: Santos (2002), p. 17, adapted.

Nuclei and Tracts

In the central nervous system, neurons often cluster into nuclei, which are groups of nerve cells that share similar functions. Tracts are bundles of nerve fibers that connect different regions of the brain or spinal cord, facilitating communication between them.

The neural structure is highly adaptable and plastic, meaning it can be modified throughout life in response to experiences, learning, and environmental demands (Santos, 2002). Neuroscientific research aims to understand the neural structure in detail, exploring its relationship with cognitive and behavioral functions, as well as how structural changes may contribute to neurological and psychiatric disorders.

Rodrigues (2022) examined multiple intelligences, identifying the brain areas activated for each. However, existential intelligence was not included in this classification. The insights from his study, which focus on other intelligences, provide valuable direction for this research and are presented in the following table:

Table 3. Types of intelligence and activated areas of the brain.

Intelligence	Description	Personalities	Activated brain areas
Logical-Mathematical	Solving logical and mathematical problems; use of deductive reasoning and calculations; related to high IQ and language; related to the original concept of intelligence and IQ, involving calculations, creation of mathematical formulas, reasoning.	Scientists, politicians, entrepreneurs, investors.	Broca's area, prefrontal cortex, left parietal lobes and temporal hemisphere and adjacent occipital association for verbal naming. Both hemispheres for spatial organization. Front system for planning and setting objectives. Associated with the level of GABA and Glutamate in the brain.
Linguistics	Verbal ability, use of words in an affective oral or written way, ease of learning languages,	Leaders, salespeople and writers.	Prefrontal cortex, Broca's area in the left inferior frontal cortex, Wernicke's area in the left temporal lobe,

	writing, reading and in rhetoric.		inferior parietal lobe, lobe and lateral sulcus (Sylvius fissure). Associated with Dopamine.
Spatial	Ability to think in three dimensions, project images with the mind, modifying them, decoding or producing them. It relates to the ability to model events and the world in a mental way, like a simulation.	Creative professionals.	Right hemisphere of the brain. The posterior parietal cortex (PPC), an area of the brain often associated with movement planning and spatial awareness, also plays a crucial role in making decisions about images in the field of view. Visual cortex, sensory cortex, parietal lobe, prefrontal cortex and cingulate cortex are able to relate to each other. Associated with high concentration of Serotonin.
Musical	Sensitivity in perceiving sounds, music, transforming them, defining them and interpreting them. In musicians, it relates to the theory of the absolute ear, that is, the ability to recognize notes just by listening	Musicians and producers.	Right hemisphere - 39% in the frontal lobe and 24% in the temporal lobe. In the parietal lobe 12%, subcortical 9% and cerebellum 8%. Motor cortex, prefrontal cortex, inferior parietal lobe, inferior frontal gyrus, and

	to their frequency. It is also related to the ability to learn and perform instruments.		superior temporal cortex. Associated with Norepinephrine and Dopamine.
Body-Kinesthetic	Use of the body to express ideas and feelings. Ability to use hands and motor coordination. It involves both body self-control and dexterity to manipulate objects, and possesses dexterity and ability to use motor skills in sports, performing or plastic arts. Here body skill, balance and motor learning are correlated.	Professions that require movement as a tool, as well as football, basketball, surgeon and dancer.	Left hemisphere, prefrontal cortex, motor area, thalamus, basal ganglia and cerebellum. Associated with Norepinephrine and Dopamine.
Interpersonal	Ability to feel empathy for people. Comprehension of facial expressions, voice, gestures, posture etc. Creation of bonds of cordiality and belonging.	Professions that work with empathy as a psychologist and psychoanalyst.	Frontal lobes, connection prefrontal cortex - limbic system. Brain regions such as the ventromedial prefrontal cortex and the orbitofrontal medial cortex, related to the processes with which the brain evaluates

			something, are related to empathy. Associated with Oxytocin (OXI) and GABA.
Intrapersonal	Construction of own evaluation with accuracy. Reflection, self-understanding and self-esteem. The opposite, when there is no intrapersonal intelligence, you may be more likely to acquire conditions of depression and other disorders.	-	Standard mode network - frontal lobe (prefrontal cortex), limbic system and insula. Associated with Dopamine and Serotonin.
Naturalist	Classification, differentiation and use of the environment. Observation, reflection and consideration about the environment. It is related to belonging, the association between one's own body and nature in general.	Biologists, veterinarians and naturalists. It is possible that painters and draftsmen may have this well-developed intelligence, facilitating the work of observation and transfer of memory lapses, translating into drawing through the motor cortex.	Prefrontal cortex, left parietal lobe to discriminate between living and non-living beings and occipital lobe. Associated with Serotonin.

Source: Own elaboration based on information from Rodrigues (2022)

General Intelligence and Brain Networks

General intelligence is not associated with a single region of the brain but is instead formed by a network of brain connections that communicate through white matter. This structure is known as the parietal-frontal network, which includes the dorsolateral prefrontal cortex, parietal lobe, anterior cingulate cortex, and several regions of the temporal and occipital lobes (Rodrigues, 2022; Goriounova & Mansvelder, 2019).

The taxonomy of general intelligence consists of fluid intelligence, crystallized intelligence, memory and learning, visual perception, auditory perception, information retrieval ability, cognitive speed, and information processing speed (Colom, Karama, et al., 2010).

- **Fluid intelligence** is linked to the lateral prefrontal cortex and parietal lobe, primarily activating the left hemisphere, with the posterior cortex playing a central role (Rodrigues, Wagner & Barth, 2022).

- **Crystallized intelligence** is associated with the temporal lobe, particularly the parahippocampal cortex (Zamroziewicz, Paul, et al., 2016).

- **Memory and learning** involve the medial temporal lobe, striatum, neocortex, amygdala, and cerebellum (Spencer, Waters, et al., 2008).

- **Visual perception** engages the frontal and parietal regions, along with the visual cortex in the occipital region (Ganis, Thompson & Kosslyn, 2004).

- **Auditory perception** is linked to the auditory cortex, with the frontal region contributing to auditory awareness and the inferior temporal cortex playing a role (Brancucci, Franciotti, et al., 2011).

- **Information retrieval ability** is associated with the medial prefrontal cortex, left parietal lobe, hippocampus, amygdala, and cerebellum (Friedman, Nessler & Johnson Jr, 2007).

- **Cognitive speed and information processing speed** are primarily influenced by white matter, which is essential for high-performance connectivity between brain regions. The left posterior parietal lobe plays a key role in this function (Turken, Whitfield-Gabrieli & Bammer, 2008).

The Triarchic Theory of Intelligence

Rodrigues (2022) also described the triarchic theory of intelligence, which categorizes intelligence into three major groups: practical, creative, and analytical.

- **Practical intelligence** refers to the ability to interact successfully with the external world and everyday life. It closely resembles naturalistic, intrapersonal, interpersonal, and logical intelligences.

o **Brain regions involved:** Occipital lobe, limbic system, prefrontal cortex.

o **Key neurotransmitters:** Dopamine, norepinephrine, serotonin.

- **Creative intelligence** applies internalized knowledge to generate new solutions. It aligns with linguistic, auditory, naturalistic, and musical intelligences.

    o **Brain regions involved:** Frontal (prefrontal cortex), parietal, occipital, and limbic areas.

    o **Key neurotransmitters:** Dopamine, norepinephrine, serotonin.

- **Analytical intelligence** is associated with high IQ and logical problem-solving.

    o **Brain regions involved:** Broca's center, prefrontal cortex, left parietal lobe, temporal hemisphere, occipital area.

    o **Key neurotransmitters:** GABA, glutamate.

Neurotransmitters and Intelligence

Rodrigues (2022) further explored how neurotransmitters facilitate intelligence by influencing cognitive functions:

- **Dopamine** is released by the ventral tegmental area and reaches the reward system through interaction with the cortical region, guiding decisions toward high-value goals.

- **Serotonin** is synthesized in the raphe nucleus and travels through the central nervous system (CNS), promoting well-being, positive emotions, and enhanced learning speed.

- **Norepinephrine** is produced in the brainstem and regulates key functions such as attention, memory, and blood pressure.

- Other essential neurotransmitters include acetylcholine, glutamate, and GABA, all of which play crucial roles in brain activity.

Despite neurotransmitters reacting naturally to stimuli, intelligent individuals can consciously or unconsciously modulate their brain interactions to their advantage.

Existential Intelligence and Brain Functions

When analyzing existential intelligence, Gardner (2006a) hesitated to classify it as a fully recognized intelligence due to the lack of direct evidence linking specific brain regions to deep existential questioning. He hypothesized that the inferotemporal lobe might contain regions crucial for processing profound existential matters. Gardner also speculated on the possibility of an existential intelligence residing deep within the temporal lobes.

The temporal lobes are essential brain regions responsible for auditory perception, memory, language processing, and emotional regulation. The inferotemporal lobe, located near the base of the brain, plays a vital role in visual recognition and long-term memory.

By comparing Gardner's preliminary analysis with Rodrigues' (2022) research and considering that existential intelligence encompasses philosophical reflection, self-awareness, and a deep understanding of existence, it is inferred that multiple brain regions may be involved, including:

- **Prefrontal Cortex:** Responsible for planning, decision-making, self-control, and introspection.

- **Cingulate Cortex:** Plays a role in cognitive conflict monitoring, emotional regulation, error processing, and self-awareness.

- **Temporal Cortex:** Particularly the **medial temporal lobe**, which is involved in memory, social cognition, and deep semantic processing.

- **Parietal Cortex:** Associated with spatial perception, sensory processing, attention, and the sense of personal identity.

- **Amygdala and Hippocampus:** Key structures for processing emotions, emotional memories, and significant life events.

- **Occipital Cortex:** Primarily involved in visual processing, which may contribute to interpreting complex abstract concepts.

It is essential to recognize that cognition, intelligence, and self-reflection are highly intricate processes involving dynamic interactions across multiple brain regions.

In a surprising hypothesis, Crick and Clark (1994) identified the anterior cingulate—specifically the anterior cingulate sulcus—as a probable candidate for the center of free will in humans. Crick based this suggestion on examinations of patients with specific injuries that appeared to interfere with their independent sense of will, such as those suffering from alien hand syndrome.

The anterior cingulate cortex is located in the frontal region of the brain and is involved in higher-level functions such as attention allocation, reward anticipation, decision-making, ethics and morality, impulse control (e.g., performance monitoring and error detection), and emotion (Rodrigues, 2022).

Allman et al. (2006) proposed that the anterior cingulate cortex is a specialization of the neocortex rather than a more primitive stage of cortical evolution. Functions central to intelligent behavior—such as emotional self-control, focused problem-solving, error recognition, and adaptive responses to changing conditions—are closely linked to emotional regulation within this framework. Evidence supporting the role of the anterior cingulate cortex in these functions has been accumulated through single-neuron recording, electrical stimulation, EEG, PET, fMRI, and injury studies.

The anterior cingulate cortex contains a class of spindle-shaped neurons found only in humans and great apes, constituting a recent evolutionary specialization likely related to these cognitive functions. Spindle cells appear to be broadly connected to various brain regions and may play a crucial role in coordination, which is essential for developing the ability to focus on complex problems. Additionally, these neurons emerge during the postnatal period, and their survival may be enhanced or diminished by environmental factors such as enrichment or stress, potentially influencing an individual's emotional self-control and problem-solving abilities in adulthood.

The anterior cingulate cortex is particularly engaged when effortful cognitive tasks are required, such as during early learning and problem-solving.

At the cellular level, the anterior cingulate cortex is unique in its abundance of specialized neurons called spindle cells, or von Economo neurons. These cells, which are a relatively recent evolutionary development, are found only in humans, other primates, cetaceans, and elephants, reinforcing the idea that this brain region is highly specialized for handling complex cognitive challenges (Allman, Hakeem, et al., 2006).

Given its role in free will, ethics, morality, problem-solving, adaptive responses to change, and the ability to focus on complex problems, the anterior cingulate cortex may be a strong candidate for addressing existential questions.

Despite the extensive mapping of brain areas presented in this work, further research—particularly involving laboratory experiments and magnetic resonance imaging—is necessary to precisely delineate how the brain engages in existential intelligence.

Development Trajectory

"It should have a distinct development trajectory. That is, different intelligences must develop at different rates and along different paths."

Different forms of intelligence develop uniquely, each following its own trajectory. This suggests that individuals should not be expected to develop all forms of intelligence in the same manner or at the same pace.

The development of existential intelligence often begins with curiosity and an interest in philosophical questions. This can emerge at any age but frequently occurs during adolescence or young adulthood when individuals begin to deeply question the world around them and seek answers to existential concerns.

However, according to Gardner (2006a), in societies where questioning is encouraged, children raise existential questions from an early age, though they may not always listen carefully to the answers. Additionally, myths and fairy tales can spark an early fascination with existential themes. Childhood exposure to fairy tales read by parents, illustrated books, and certain children's films can stimulate interest in these profound questions.

The study of philosophy, literature, religion, and ethics plays a significant role in the development of existential intelligence. This involves reading works by renowned philosophers, exploring existentialist literature and religious texts, and examining diverse perspectives on moral and ethical dilemmas.

Often, this form of intelligence develops through personal reflection and deep contemplation. Individuals engage in moments of introspection, pondering the purpose of their own lives, their values, and the significance of their experiences.

Engaging in meaningful dialogue with others who share philosophical or existential interests can be highly enriching. Such discussions encourage the exchange of ideas, challenge existing beliefs, and expand one's understanding of existential issues.

As individuals encounter life challenges, experience major changes, and face pivotal moments, they may gain a deeper understanding of existential questions. Personal experiences—such as the loss of a loved one or a near-death experience (NDE)—can lead to profound reflections on mortality and the impermanence of life. This type of contemplation was notably prevalent during the COVID-19 pandemic.

The search for meaning and purpose in life is central to existential intelligence. This pursuit can influence career choices, inspire participation in volunteer work, or prompt a deeper engagement with spiritual or religious practices.

On the other hand, an agnostic individual studying the universe and cosmology might find that science offers powerful avenues for developing existential intelligence—demonstrating that this intelligence is not necessarily tied to spiritual or religious beliefs.

Existential intelligence is a continuously evolving process. As individuals mature and accumulate life experiences, their perspectives on existential matters can shift and deepen.

It is important to note that the development of existential intelligence is unique to each person and can occur at various stages of life. Furthermore, not everyone cultivates this intelligence to the same degree, as it depends on personal interests, motivations, and opportunities for learning. Nonetheless, developing existential intelligence can lead to a richer, more meaningful life.

This intelligence appears to develop at a distinct pace, independent of other intelligences, following its own path of evolution.

Evolutionary Biology

"It must have some basis in evolutionary biology. In other words, an intelligence must have a prior instantiation in primates or other species and putative survival value."

The notion of "existential intelligence" is not widely recognized in evolutionary biology or any other scientific field. Instead, intelligence is typically discussed in terms of cognitive abilities— the capacity to learn, solve problems, adapt to the environment, and make complex decisions.

Discovering Existential Intelligence

The evolution of cognitive intelligence remains a topic of ongoing research and debate within evolutionary biology. The leading theory explaining the development of intelligence in living organisms is Charles Darwin's theory of natural selection. According to this theory, intelligence evolved due to selective pressures, meaning individuals with traits that enhanced their ability to survive and reproduce had an evolutionary advantage.

However, cognitive intelligence did not emerge suddenly in a single species. Rather, different aspects of intelligence, such as learning and problem-solving abilities, are believed to have evolved gradually across various species. Primates, including humans, are known for their advanced cognitive capacities compared to many other species. However, there is no recognized "prior instantiation" of existential intelligence in primates or any other species within the scientific literature.

A species' survival and reproductive success are often linked to its ability to adapt to its environment and overcome specific challenges. As a result, cognitive intelligence, in its many forms, may have been favored by natural selection in multiple species, including primates. Nonetheless, intelligence is a highly complex and multifaceted trait, influenced by various factors such as ecology, diet, and social interactions.

In summary, existential intelligence is not a commonly acknowledged concept in evolutionary biology. Instead, the evolution of intelligence is generally discussed in terms of cognitive intelligence, which likely developed in multiple species through natural selection and other evolutionary processes.

Tracing the Possible Emergence of Existential Intelligence

Despite these limitations, we will explore the key evolutionary achievements of our ancestors that may provide early indications of the emergence of existential intelligence in ancient times.

According to Becoming Human (2023), the first known inventions of our ancestors were stone tools. These tools enabled hominids to access bone marrow and process meat and other food, marking a cognitive leap, as very few animals are capable of making and using tools. The earliest stone tools, discovered at Lomekwi, date back approximately 3.4 million years. Additionally, animal bones with butchering marks have been found at Dikika, slightly younger at around 3.3 million years old.

Around 2 million years ago, hominids of the genus Homo began developing a remarkable adaptation—larger brains. All primates possess relatively large brains in proportion to their body size, but the expansion seen in early Pleistocene hominids (2.5 million to 780,000 years ago) far exceeded that of other primates. Larger brains require more energy, meaning these early hominids needed higher-calorie, nutrient-rich diets to sustain their neural development. This trend toward increased brain size and enhanced cognition laid the foundation for the evolution of modern humans, making our species the most intellectually advanced and dominant life form on Earth (Becoming Human, 2023).

For millions of years, our ancestors lived, evolved, and survived on the African continent, where our species eventually emerged. While the environments, ecosystems, and pressures shaping their lives varied across time and space, Africa remains the birthplace of our lineage. Fossil evidence indicates that early hominids ventured beyond Africa at least 1.8 million years ago. These early explorers, belonging to the species Homo erectus, migrated out of Africa in several waves. Fossils of Homo erectus discovered in Dmanisi, Georgia, date back to 1.8 million years ago, suggesting that migration began even earlier. The exact reasons for their movement remain uncertain, but it is possible that they followed migrating animal herds (Becoming Human, 2023).

If this theory holds, then by tracking migrating herds, Homo erectus may have begun to grasp the vastness of the world beyond their familiar surroundings. Alternatively, they might have embarked on migration due to their own curiosity, seeking out the unknown. Either scenario could indicate the earliest seeds of existential intelligence—an awareness of a world beyond their immediate experience.

The Use of Fire and Early Existential Thought

Evidence of sporadic fire use appears in the archaeological record as early as 1.5 million years ago, with burnt sediments preserved in ancient sites. Initially, fire may have been naturally ignited by lightning. However, controlled use of fire, with designated hearths, only appears around 800,000 years ago. Fire provided significant survival advantages, including warmth, protection from predators, illumination, and the ability to cook food. While meat consumption was already a crucial part of hominid evolution, the controlled use of fire for cooking did not emerge until about 120,000 years ago. Cooking increased the bioavailability of nutrients, simplified food processing, and helped eliminate pathogens from meat (Becoming Human, 2023).

This raises a compelling question: before learning to control fire, did hominids ever wonder about its origins? Did witnessing lightning strikes and subsequent fires spark curiosity about their cause? If so, this period could represent another milestone in the development of existential intelligence—early humans questioning the forces of nature and their place in the world.

The discovery of heat-treated and flaked stone tools in southern Africa, dated to around 70,000 years ago, suggests that early humans' ability to solve complex problems may have developed alongside their modern genetic lineage. At this time, they were benefiting from the abundant and predictable marine food resources along the coast. Soft stones called silcrete had to undergo heat treatment to harden them for flint knapping. If the stones were overheated, they became brittle; if not heated enough, they failed to break sharply. This intricate process indicates that early modern humans living in caves at the southernmost point of Africa possessed the cognitive ability to replicate this technique and likely passed their knowledge on to others in their group (Becoming Human 2023).

The capacity to solve complex problems also connects to the profound questions posed by existential intelligence, which involves the ability to think beyond convention and seek innovative answers or solutions.

Between 250,000 and 50,000 years ago, the first burials appeared, roughly aligning with the Middle Paleolithic period (250,000 to 30,000 years ago) in Eurasia. Skeletal remains from the Middle Stone Age in Africa, attributed to early Homo sapiens, show some form of post-mortem modification, though most cannot be classified as formal burials. One exception is Border Cave 3. Additionally, a skull from Herto, Ethiopia, dating back roughly 160,000 years, displays modifications to its bone surface. The earliest known modern human burials come from Lake Mungo, Australia, where a shallow pit burial and cremated remains of another individual date to around 40,000 years ago. In Europe, some of the earliest Upper Paleolithic burials (50,000 to 10,000 years ago) were found in the caves of Mladec, Czech Republic, approximately 31,000 years ago. The well-known Cro-Magnon burials, considered synonymous with early modern humans, date to about 28,000 years ago in the Cro-Magnon rock shelter in France (Becoming Human 2023).

Burial practices held profound cultural and spiritual significance for many ancient societies, often reflecting beliefs about the afterlife, the soul, and the individual's role within the community. The act of burying the dead forces a society to confront fundamental questions about human existence, purpose, and the possibility of life after death. This may serve as another early indication of the emergence of existential intelligence.

The written records left by the first civilizations, approximately 5,400 years ago, provide valuable insight into their daily lives, worldview, and cultural developments. The first known culture to develop writing was the Mesopotamians, who used a pictographic script called cuneiform. This writing system, inscribed on clay tablets with a stylus made from dried reeds, enabled humans to express ideas across time and space. Writing allowed information to be transmitted indirectly, facilitating widespread knowledge-sharing and the accumulation of wisdom across generations and cultures (Becoming Human 2023).

This ability to pass down ideas through written language demonstrates a concern for the future and the legacy left behind—an aspect closely tied to existential intelligence.

In summary, while the concept of "existential intelligence" is not widely recognized in scientific disciplines, intelligence is generally examined in cognitive terms. The evolution of cognitive intelligence is a well-discussed topic, with Charles Darwin's theory of natural selection providing a framework for its development. However, the emergence of existential intelligence remains a more speculative and intricate subject. Archaeological findings offer glimpses of its potential origins, such as technological innovations, territorial expansions, fire domestication, and the first burial practices, which suggest early reflections on the afterlife. These milestones highlight the increasing complexity of human cognition and its inclination toward deep existential inquiry. Nonetheless, understanding existential intelligence remains an ongoing challenge, open to reinterpretation and debate as new discoveries shed light on the mysteries of human history.

Capture in Symbol Systems

"It should be susceptible to capture in symbol systems, of the kind used in formal or informal education."

To say that a form of intelligence must be susceptible to capture in symbol systems—such as those used in formal or informal education—means that it should be expressible, comprehensible, and teachable through symbolic representations. These symbols include words, numbers, graphs, mathematical notations, diagrams, and other forms of structured language.

This implies that the intelligence in question can be systematically communicated and transmitted to others in an organized manner. Capturing intelligence within symbol systems is fundamental to education, enabling knowledge and skills to be passed from one generation to the next, from teachers to students, and from various sources of information to learners.

Mathematics serves as an excellent example of intelligence that is well captured in symbol systems. Mathematical concepts, ranging from basic arithmetic to advanced calculations, are expressed through symbols and formulas that can be taught in classrooms, documented in textbooks, and disseminated in a structured manner. Students learn to use these symbols to solve problems, perform calculations, and understand abstract theories.

Similarly, language is another form of intelligence that is effectively represented through symbol systems. Written language allows for the structured transmission of ideas, narratives, and information, ensuring continuity across cultures and generations.

However, not all forms of intelligence lend themselves equally to symbolic representation. Some types of knowledge or skills are more challenging to capture and convey through symbols. For example, emotional intelligence—encompassing the ability to recognize, understand, and manage one's own emotions as well as those of others—is not as easily expressed in formal systems, although emotional skills can still be developed and taught through contextual and experiential learning.

In conclusion, the ability to encapsulate intelligence within symbol systems is crucial for its effective communication and instruction, particularly in educational settings. Nevertheless, some forms of intelligence are more easily structured and transmitted through symbols than others, highlighting the importance of diverse approaches in education and human development.

When it comes to existential intelligence— which involves deep reflection on fundamental questions of human existence, such as the purpose of life, death, and philosophical inquiry— its capture in symbol systems is more challenging compared to traditional forms of cognitive intelligence. However, aspects of existential intelligence can still be addressed and taught in both formal and informal educational contexts through a multidisciplinary and tailored approach. Below are some examples:

Philosophy and Ethics

Existential intelligence often relates to philosophical and ethical issues. Courses in philosophy, ethics, and religious studies provide a platform to explore these profound questions. Students can read philosophical texts, analyze ethical dilemmas, and engage in discussions about existential topics.

Literature and the Arts

Literature, poetry, and the arts frequently explore existential themes. Studying literary and artistic works that address deep human concerns can help students reflect on these themes and express their own ideas through writing and artistic creation.

Interdisciplinary Studies

Interdisciplinary educational programs can integrate fields such as philosophy, psychology, religion, literature, and sociology to explore existential questions in a comprehensive manner.

Meditation and Mindfulness

Practicing meditation and mindfulness fosters self-awareness and contemplation. These practices can be incorporated into educational programs to encourage reflection and introspection.

Group Discussions

Facilitating open discussions about existential issues can effectively engage students. Open dialogue and debate help explore different perspectives and deepen their understanding of existential questions.

Personal Narratives

Encouraging students to write personal narratives about their existential experiences and reflections allows them to express their own journeys and understandings symbolically.

Counseling and Guidance

Trained professionals in counseling and mentoring can play a crucial role in both formal and informal education by providing support and guidance to individuals exploring personal existential issues.

Multimedia Resources

Educational tools such as videos, podcasts, and presentations can effectively convey concepts and ideas related to existential intelligence.

It is important to recognize that existential intelligence is highly individualized and subjective. There are no definitive answers to many of the questions it raises. The goal is not necessarily to find absolute truths but to promote reflection, exploration, and the pursuit of personal meaning. Educational approaches must be sensitive to students' individual beliefs and values, while respecting diverse existential perspectives.

Psychometric Tests to Measure Existential Intelligence

"It should be supported by evidence from psychometric intelligence tests."

Since Gardner introduced the idea of existential intelligence, several researchers have developed tests to measure it, some even submitting their work to Gardner himself. In a blog post (Gardner, 2020), he mentioned that he would provide feedback if someone sent him a test for evaluation.

Allan and Shearer (2012) developed the **Scale for Existential Thinking** (SET), which measures an individual's tendency to explore fundamental concerns of human existence and engage in meaning-making. The psychometric properties of the SET, composed of 11 items, were evaluated in two studies, demonstrating a one-dimensional factor structure and strong reliability in both student and adult samples. The SET also showed construct validity through correlations with measures of life meaning, curiosity, and other existential variables.

Jaddou (2018) examined existential intelligence among students at the World Islamic Sciences University in Jordan using an adapted version of the existential intelligence scale originally developed by

Zubi et al. (2015). This scale was derived from Allan and Shearer's SET (2012).

Sharma and Jha (2021) developed the **Existential Thinking Capacity Scale** (ETAS), an 18-item questionnaire using a 5-point Likert scale. Professors from Indian universities validated the scale, and Howard Gardner himself reviewed it. The researchers incorporated suggestions from Gardner and university professors, refining the scale's language and dimensions. The ETAS was found to be one-dimensional, with a Cronbach's alpha reliability coefficient of $\alpha = .84$ (determined using SPSS). However, the scale itself could not be located through online searches, as the published article only contained analyses and results without the questionnaire.

The researchers noted a limitation in their study: the test was conducted exclusively on an Indian population, whose cultural and religious perspectives may differ significantly from those of other regions. They cautioned that the ETAS should be used with care when applied in diverse cultural contexts.

Fernandes (2021) proposed the **Existential Intelligence Scale** (EIS) to assess an individual's ability to engage in introspection about essential existential themes, such as death, origins, and the nature of reality. The EIS, composed of 12 items, was designed in response to the author's dissatisfaction with previous existential scales. Fernandes sought to create a more comprehensive and precise assessment of existential intelligence. More details on this study can be found in the Theoretical Framework.

These examples demonstrate that researchers have made methodological attempts to measure existential intelligence. However, most tests are based on international literature and have been developed under the cultural influence of specific countries, without being widely replicated across different populations. Additionally, some assessments incorporate elements of spiritual intelligence or fail to evaluate existential intelligence in a singular and complete manner.

To address these limitations, it is necessary to develop a scale for existential intelligence in **Portuguese**, for Brazilian people, for example, taking into account national cultural contexts. This new scale should integrate the strengths of existing assessments while ensuring a more comprehensive and replicable approach.

Despite these challenges, existing psychometric tests indicate that existential intelligence can be identified and measured within study groups.

Experimental Psychological Tasks

"It must be distinguishable from other intelligences by experimental psychological tasks."

McKenzie (1999) developed the Multiple Intelligence Inventory, which consists of nine sections, each corresponding to a specific intelligence domain. This inventory measures the level of each intelligence type, allowing for differentiation among various modalities. Each section contains ten statements that respondents must evaluate. If a statement accurately describes them, they mark it with a "1." If they do not identify with a statement, they leave the space blank. At the end of the questionnaire, the total for each section is summed.

Ramos and Martins (2018) conducted research on the adoption of digital screens and new technological tools in educational settings, examining how these innovations engage different intelligences. Their study aimed to identify how multiple intelligences are exercised when using digital games for educational purposes. A questionnaire was administered to 58 students enrolled in the Extension Course in Continuing Education in School Councils. The results showed that intelligence related to mathematics and logical reasoning was the most utilized, followed by existential intelligence, abstraction, spatial intelligence, and motor coordination.

Regarding existential intelligence, students were asked whether they encountered ethical and moral dilemmas during gameplay, allowing researchers to assess this domain of intelligence. This study suggests that existential intelligence can be distinguished from other modalities.

A study by Ayasrah and Aljarrah (2020) sought to identify differences in multiple intelligences among students at Jordan University of Science and Technology, examining correlations with gender, academic year, and performance. The study involved 349 participants of both sexes and utilized the MacKenzie Scale for Multiple Intelligences.

The researchers concluded that cultural, religious, and societal traditions influenced the expression of existential and musical intelligences. They noted that the university lacked the necessary tools, spaces, and methods to foster the development of these intelligence types.

In addition to these studies, several experiments measuring existential intelligence in specific interest groups have been referenced in this work, including research by Jaddou (2018), Fernandes (2021), Adi Astuti et al. (2021), Sharma and Jha (2021), and Paramasivam et al. (2022).

Based on these studies, it is evident that existential intelligence is distinguishable from other forms of intelligence through experimental psychological tasks.

Central Information Processing System

"It must demonstrate a central information processing system. That is, there must be identifiable mental processes that deal with information related to each intelligence."

The concept of a Central Information Processing System (CIPS) suggests the existence of a structure or mechanism within an intelligent entity responsible for processing information, storing knowledge, making inferences, and facilitating decision-making. In humans, this system is represented by the brain and nervous system, which process sensory information, memories, thoughts, and environmental data, enabling cognitive tasks and choices.

Identifiable mental processes refer to the cognitive, emotional, and perceptual mechanisms occurring within the CIPS, which can be studied and analyzed.

Some examples of these processes include:

Perception: The processing of sensory information to interpret the environment, including sight, hearing, smell, taste, and touch.

Memory: The storage and retrieval of past experiences for future use.

Thinking: The process of reasoning, problem-solving, and decision-making.

Emotion: Emotional responses to stimuli or events that can influence thoughts and behavior.

Learning: The acquisition of new knowledge and skills through experience or study.

Each type of intelligence—whether human, animal, artificial, or otherwise—has its own set of identifiable mental processes and a unique CIPS that allows it to function. The complexity and efficiency of these processes vary depending on the nature of the intelligence in question.

For existential intelligence, its CIPS would be responsible for processing information related to existential, philosophical, and meaning-oriented inquiries. This system could include:

Philosophical Reflection: The ability to contemplate profound existential questions, such as the purpose of life, the nature of consciousness, morality, and other philosophical topics.

Self-Awareness and Self-Reflection: The capacity to recognize one's own thoughts, emotions, and experiences, as well as to reflect on the significance of one's existence.

Understanding the Existential Context: The ability to place one's own life within a broader framework, including an awareness of mortality, human connections, and the search for meaning.

Existential Decision-Making: The ability to make life-altering choices, such as career decisions, the adoption of core values, and the formation of personal beliefs.

Pursuit of Meaning and Purpose: The intrinsic motivation to seek deeper meaning in life and establish a personal sense of purpose that extends beyond fulfilling basic needs.

Conclusion

Based on the application of the criteria for identifying an intelligence, as established by **Gardner (1983)** and **Kornhaber, Fierros, & Veneema (2004)**, it can be concluded that:

i. It may be observed in relative isolation among prodigies or other exceptional populations.

ii. Although this work attempted to map the areas of the brain activated by existential intelligence, further research involving laboratory experiments and magnetic resonance imaging is necessary to precisely determine how the brain functions in relation to this domain of intelligence.

iii. This intelligence develops at a different pace than other intelligences, evolving independently without being directly linked to their development. It follows distinct pathways in its progression.

iv. Through archaeological findings and historical evidence, researchers can uncover clues about the emergence and evolution of existential intelligence. However, fully understanding it remains a challenge, subject to ongoing interpretation and debate.

v. Capturing existential intelligence within symbolic systems is more complex compared to traditional forms of cognitive intelligence. Nevertheless, aspects of existential intelligence can still be addressed and taught in both formal and informal educational settings through a multidisciplinary and tailored approach.

vi. Some researchers have developed psychometric tests to identify and measure existential intelligence in study groups. However, these tests have limitations when applied in Brazil, requiring careful review for the development of an existential intelligence scale in Portuguese.

vii. Several studies have demonstrated that existential intelligence is distinguishable from other forms of intelligence through experimental psychological tasks.

viii. Its Central Information Processing System would be responsible for analyzing information related to existential, philosophical, and meaning-oriented questions of life.

Characteristics of an Individual with a High Level of Existential Intelligence

An individual with a high level of existential intelligence demonstrates profound reflection and understanding of philosophical, metaphysical, and existential issues. While there is no single definition or consensus on what constitutes existential intelligence, some common characteristics include:

- **Deep Reflection:** Individuals with high existential intelligence engage in profound contemplation about fundamental aspects of life, such as the purpose of existence, the nature of reality, and mortality.

- **Meaning-Seeking:** They constantly search for meaning and purpose in their lives and the world around them. They question the status quo and do not accept superficial answers to existential questions.

- **Awareness of Mortality:** These individuals often confront the reality of death more directly and deeply than most people. This awareness can lead to a greater appreciation of life and a desire to live meaningfully.

- **Openness to Ambiguity:** They are more likely to embrace uncertainty, recognizing that many existential questions do not have definitive answers. They are comfortable with the complexity and multifaceted nature of life.

- **Critical Thinking:** Existential intelligence is often associated with strong analytical skills and the ability to evaluate complex issues logically and rationally.

- **Empathy and Compassion:** Those with high existential intelligence tend to have a deep understanding of human struggles, making them more empathetic and compassionate toward others.

- **Intellectual Curiosity:** They exhibit an insatiable curiosity about philosophical and existential questions and are open to exploring different perspectives and schools of thought.

- **Creativity:** Existential intelligence is often linked to creativity, as individuals who explore deep issues are frequently capable of generating original ideas and innovative approaches to problems.

- **Authenticity:** They tend to be genuine and true to themselves in their actions and relationships, striving to live in accordance with their convictions and values, even if it means challenging societal norms.

- **Acceptance of Finitude:** They acknowledge the impermanence of life, which leads them to value the time they have and make choices that align with their deepest values and goals.

It is important to note that existential intelligence is complex, and not all individuals who exhibit these traits do so in the same way. Additionally, possessing existential intelligence does not necessarily correlate with happiness or success, as it can sometimes lead to greater existential distress and emotional challenges.

Analysis of Existing Psychometric Questionnaires

Since existential intelligence deals with complex and abstract aspects of human cognition, designing an accurate and reliable test to measure it can be challenging. Most traditional intelligence tests focus on more quantifiable and well-defined cognitive skills, such as linguistic, mathematical, or spatial reasoning, which are easier to objectively assess than an individual's ability to contemplate the meaning of life while staring into a cup of coffee.

To address this challenge, it is essential to critically examine previous tests from the literature that have attempted to measure existential intelligence.

Scale for Existential Thinking (Allan & Shearer, 2012)

This scale consists of 11 questions designed to assess existential thought processes. The response format follows a six-point Likert scale, ranging from *rarely* to *all the time*, with an additional *I don't know* option.

Table 4 - Scale for Existential Thinking

1. Have you ever contemplated your life's purpose?

2. Have you ever pondered the human spirit or what happens after death?

3. Have you spent time reading, thinking about, or discussing philosophy or belief systems?

4. Do you have a personal philosophy that helps you navigate stress or make significant life decisions?

5. Do you reflect on concepts such as eternity, truth, justice, and goodness?

6. Do you engage in meditation, prayer, or deep reflection on life's mysteries?

7. Do you explore or ask profound questions to better understand the meaning of life?

8. Have you ever considered a "grand design" or overarching process that humanity is a part of?

9. Do you think about what exists beyond the immediate "here and now" of daily life?

10. Have you ever reflected on life's fundamental questions?

11. Have you ever contemplated the nature of reality or the universe?

Source: Allan & Shearer, 2012.

Key Observations:

The scale effectively addresses fundamental existential concerns, such as life purpose, meaning, and philosophical reflection.

However, some questions incorporate religious or spiritual language (e.g., "human spirit," "prayer"), which may introduce bias. This is because an agnostic person involved in the study of the universe and cosmology may argue that science also provides profound avenues for developing existential intelligence, without necessarily being tied to spiritual beliefs.

For example, two agnostic French philosophers, previously mentioned in this work, demonstrate a high level of existential intelligence. One of them, Jean-Paul Sartre, argued that existence precedes essence and that human beings are free to create their own meaning in life, independent of religious belief.

Another notable French philosopher, existentialist and agnostic, was Albert Camus. He explored the idea that life is inherently absurd and that one cannot derive a transcendental meaning from it, including belief in God.

Therefore, to ensure a neutral and inclusive approach, it is recommended that such terms be replaced with more philosophically neutral wording (e.g., replacing "spirituality" with "sense of existence").

Adapted Scale for Existential Thinking (Zubi et al., 2015)

An adaptation of Allan & Shearer's scale, this version expands to 20 questions and integrates additional existential themes.

Table 5 - Adapted Scale for Existential Thinking

1. Do you think more about reality or about people?
2. Do you discover philosophical ideas through literature or works of art?
3. Do you engage in discussions about philosophical questions and attempt to answer them?
4. Do you discuss religious topics that have no definitive answers?
5. Do you spend time in prayer?
6. Do you seek in-depth answers to life's fundamental questions?
7. Do those close to you believe that you have a deep understanding of life's essential issues?
8. Do you contemplate concepts such as eternity, honesty, justice, and kindness?
9. Do you spend time reflecting on the mysteries of the universe?
10. Do you often mediate conflicts between people around you?
11. Are you consistently working toward your goals?
12. Do you think about the concept of the soul or spirit?
13. Do you spend time discussing a specific philosophy or belief system?
14. Do you dedicate time to reading and deep thinking?

15. Do you reflect on what happens to us after death?

16. Do you believe there is life on other planets?

17. Have you ever contemplated the meaning or secret of life?

18. Do you believe in the existence of ghosts?

19. Have you reflected on human suffering and its causes?

20. Have you ever considered the origins of humanity?

Source: Zubi et al., 2015

Key Observations:

The addition of extra items expands the scale's scope but also introduces ambiguities. For instance, the question about mediating conflicts among those around you lacks a clear connection to existential intelligence.

Several questions retain religious undertones, including references to prayer, spirits, and ghosts. While the scale seeks to explore existential inquiry more deeply, it veers toward mysticism and religious themes, which may compromise its objectivity.

Existential Intelligence Scale (Fernandes, 2021)

Developed to overcome the limitations of earlier scales, this instrument consists of 12 items specifically designed to assess existential reflection.

Table 6 - Existential Intelligence Scale

1. I actively try to understand my purpose.
2. I am fascinated/intrigued when I hear people talk about the meaning of life or if such topics are discussed.

3. I usually read books or articles or watch videos/lectures on the meaning of life.

4. I spend a lot of time thinking about my existence or existence in general and/or its meaning.

5. I'm drawn to conversations/books/lectures/ or other platforms (podcasts, etc.) that discuss death, dying, and the afterlife.

6. I often take a break from my day to day life to think about what I'm doing or why I'm doing it.

7. I spend a lot of time thinking about what (aspect of me or in general) defines me.

8. {reverse} I don't find conversations about the universe and our conscious experience of it fascinating or even interesting.

9. I spend a lot of time contemplating whether my existence (and others) is real.

10. {reverse} I prefer not to talk or think about death or the afterlife.

11. I spend a lot of time thinking about the nature of reality and whether **God exists.**

12. I often think of the origin of existence.

Source: Fernandes, 2021
Key Observations:

This scale is more philosophically rigorous and avoids overt religious framing.

It includes reverse-coded items, which enhance reliability by minimizing response bias.

However, one question explicitly references belief in God, which may impact neutrality. Adjusting the wording could improve its applicability across diverse belief systems.

Multiple Intelligence Inventory (McKenzie, 1999)

This broader inventory assesses multiple intelligence domains. Originally composed of nine sections, only the ten questions related to existential intelligence were considered for this study.

Table 7 - Multiple Intelligence Inventory (adapted)

1. It's important to see my role in the "big picture" of things.
2. I like to discuss questions about life.
3. Religion is important to me.
4. I like to see artwork.
5. Relaxation and meditation exercises are rewarding for me.
6. I like to travel to visit inspiring places.
7. I like to read about philosophers.
8. Learning new things is easier when I see your application in the real world.
9. I wonder if there are other forms of intelligent life in the universe.
10. It's important for me to feel connected to people, ideas, and beliefs.

Source: McKenzie, 1999

Key Observations:

Unlike previous scales, this inventory incorporates lifestyle preferences (e.g., travel, art appreciation, meditation), which may reflect personality traits rather than existential intelligence.

The phrasing of certain questions (e.g., "Religion is important to me") suggests a spiritual bias.

Overall, this tool is less precise in capturing the core cognitive dimensions of existential intelligence.

Comparative Analysis & Recommendations

Each scale offers unique contributions but also presents limitations in measuring existential intelligence without religious bias.

Table 8 - Comparative Analysis

Scale	Strengths	Limitations
Allan & Shearer (2012)	Strong foundation in existential inquiry	Some religious/spiritual terms introduce bias
Zubi et al. (2015)	Broader range of existential themes	Mystical elements reduce neutrality
Fernandes (2021)	Most rigorous and philosophically neutral	One item could be reworded to avoid theological assumptions

Scale	Strengths	Limitations
McKenzie (1999)	Connects existential thought to lifestyle and behavior	More personality-driven than intelligence-based

Source: the author

Final Recommendations:

Refine Question Wording: To maintain neutrality, terms related to religion should be rephrased in a more philosophical or existential manner.

Develop a Hybrid Model: Creating a modified version that integrates the strengths of different scales could enhance validity and applicability.

Expand Response Metrics: Standardizing response formats and incorporating a justification/explanation section for certain items may help distinguish deep existential thinking from casual reflection.

Proposal of Two New Scales to Measure Existential Intelligence

To address the limitations of existing instruments and provide a more precise assessment of existential intelligence, this study proposes two new scales:

Existential Intelligence Scale for Youth and Adults (EISYA) – A 20-item scale categorized into four key domains:

Purpose

Life and the Universe

Nature of Reality

Collective Experience

Existential Intelligence Scale for Children (EISC) – A simpler, 5-item scale designed to assess existential intelligence in younger individuals, considering their cognitive development and behavioral patterns.

These scales were developed based on an extensive review of existing literature, as analyzed in the previous section, with a focus on core existential themes while avoiding overlap with other forms of intelligence. Additionally, the questions were carefully structured to be clear, non-repetitive, and free from religious or mystical bias, ensuring a neutral and inclusive measurement of existential intelligence.

Methodological Approach in Scale Development

The construction of these scales followed the principles outlined by Alexandre and Coluci (2011) regarding content validity in measurement instruments. They emphasize that content validity involves a two-stage process:

Instrument Development – Defining the construct, identifying key domains, and formulating appropriate items.

Expert Evaluation – Validating the instrument through specialist analysis before broader testing.

In this study, **The First Stage**—the development of the scales—was completed, while the expert review and validation process will be addressed in future research.

According to Lynn (1986), cognitive measures should follow these steps:

- Identification of key domains
- Construction of items
- Organization of items into a coherent scale

Following these guidelines, the domains of existential intelligence in this study were defined based on:

- Howard Gardner's (1983) multiple intelligences theory
- Research on intelligence assessment by Kornhaber, Fierros, & Veneema (2004)
- A critical analysis of existing existential intelligence questionnaires

Additionally, special attention was given to cultural adaptation when incorporating translated questions from other scales. As Alexandre and Coluci (2011) highlight, adapting a measurement tool involves more than simple translation—it requires adjustments for linguistic, cultural, and contextual relevance.

Existential Intelligence Scale for Youth and Adults (EISYA)

- This 20-item scale employs a five-point Likert scale:
- Strongly disagree
- Disagree
- Neither agree nor disagree
- Agree
- Strongly agree

The maximum possible score is 100 points (20 × 5).Reverse-scored items are adjusted accordingly, ensuring that lower scores reflect weaker existential intelligence, while higher scores indicate stronger existential engagement.

Figure 5 - Existential Intelligence Scale for Youth and Adults (EISYA)

PURPOSE

1. I actively try to understand my purpose.
2. I am intrigued by understanding the purpose of human existence.
3. I care about my physical body to have longevity and fulfill my life purpose.
4. I attribute meaning to my work, making it a tool to help fulfill my life purpose.
5. (reverse) I think that artificial intelligence can take the place of human beings and leave humanity without purpose.

LIFE AND UNIVERSE

6. I seek to reflect on the origin of the universe and life.
7. I wonder if there are other intelligent life forms in the universe.
8. I am attracted to conversations/books/lectures/ or other platforms (podcasts, etc.) that discuss death, dying and the afterlife.
9. I think about the meaning of human finitude.
10. I like reading and researching the relativity of time and the theory of multiverses.

NATURE OF REALITY

11. I often take a break from my daily life to think about what I'm doing or why I'm doing it.
12. I try to understand reality and I have asked myself whether the world around us is genuine and not an illusion.
13. I seek to understand whether we are free beings with free will or our existence is determined by causes and prior conditions.
14. I usually think about the various consequences of a decision before acting.
15. I consider all the variables within my reach to project future scenarios and plan my actions in advance.

COLLECTIVE EXPERIENCE

16. (reverse) I usually spend a lot of my time on social media.
17. I try to prioritize collective well-being over individual well-being.
18. I try to understand human suffering and its causes.
19. I question whether there is an objective basis for morality and how we should decide what is right or wrong.
20. Sometimes I come across a good argument that challenges some of my strongest beliefs.

Source: the author.

Existential Intelligence Scale for Children (EISC)

For younger participants, a simpler binary response system is used:

- 1 = Yes

- **0 = No**

Since the scale consists of five questions, the maximum possible score is **5 points**.

This format provides a clear and straightforward assessment of existential intelligence in children while ensuring that the questions remain age-appropriate and easily understandable.

Figure 6 - Existential Intelligence Scale for Children (EISC)

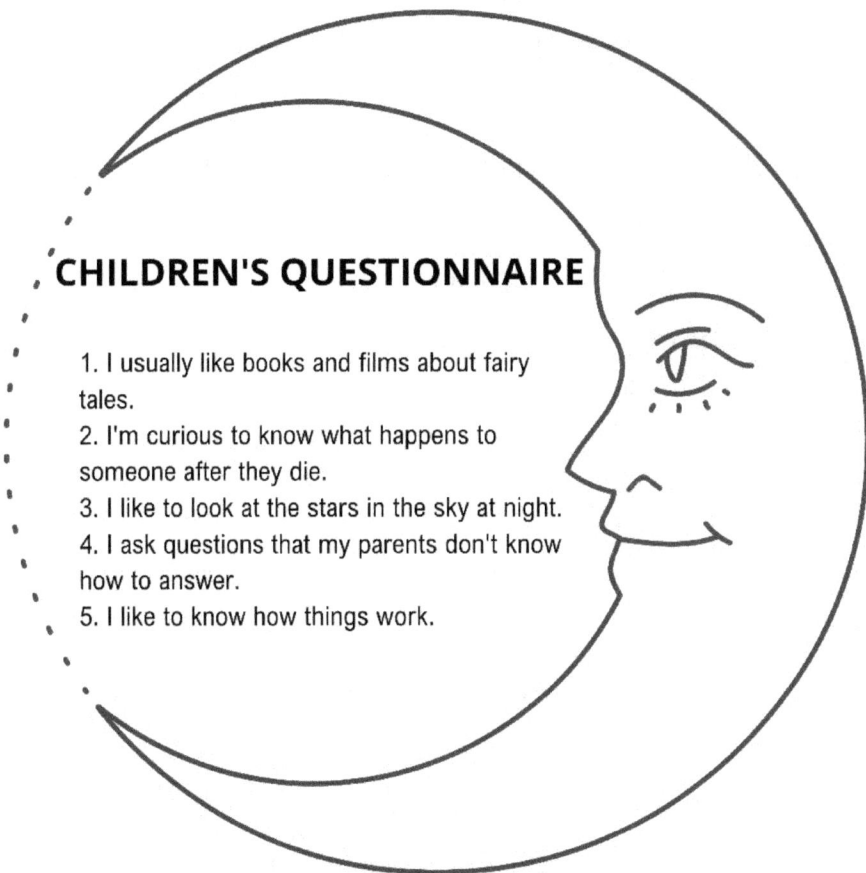

CHILDREN'S QUESTIONNAIRE

1. I usually like books and films about fairy tales.
2. I'm curious to know what happens to someone after they die.
3. I like to look at the stars in the sky at night.
4. I ask questions that my parents don't know how to answer.
5. I like to know how things work.

Source: the author.

Enhancing Existential Intelligence in the Classroom

Fostering existential intelligence in educational settings encourages students to think deeply, reflect critically, and engage meaningfully with the world around them. Educators can implement several evidence-based strategies to cultivate this form of intelligence.

1. Connecting Learning to the Bigger Picture

Relating academic content to real-world issues enhances students' understanding of how knowledge shapes human existence. For example:

- Discussions on **environmental sustainability** can link scientific principles to ethical questions about humanity's responsibility to the planet.

- **Historical studies** can explore the philosophical implications of major events.

2. Encouraging Big-Picture Thinking

Students should be guided to synthesize complex ideas and recognize how individual concepts contribute to larger frameworks. Examples include:

- Exploring **universal human experiences** through literature and philosophy.

- Analyzing **historical events** from multiple perspectives, fostering critical and abstract reasoning.

3. Promoting Multiple Viewpoints

Encouraging students to examine topics from diverse perspectives nurtures empathy and open-mindedness. Possible activities:

- **Structured debates** on ethical dilemmas.
- **Role-playing exercises** to explore different worldviews.

4. Reflection and Synthesis Exercises

Students benefit from summarizing and analyzing their thoughts through:

- **Reflective journaling**
- **Concept mapping**
- **Oral presentations** on existential themes

These activities help consolidate learning while reinforcing the importance of deep reflection.

5. Peer-to-Peer Teaching Opportunities

Encouraging students to explain complex ideas to their classmates strengthens both understanding and engagement. Activities may include:

- **Student-led discussions** on existential topics.
- **Collaborative group projects** that explore existential themes.

The Role of Educators in Developing Existential Intelligence

According to Howard Gardner (2006a), existential intelligence is a natural trait in children that should be nurtured rather than overlooked. In societies that encourage questioning, children naturally engage in existential inquiry, asking profound questions about life, purpose, and the universe.

Teachers play a critical role in fostering this innate curiosity by:

- Encouraging students to ask **existential questions** without fear of "wrong" answers.

- Providing **resources and discussions** that help students explore meaningful topics.

- Designing **assignments** that challenge students to engage with deep, philosophical issues.

Using the EISC as an Educational Tool

The **Existential Intelligence Scale for Children (EISC)** serves as a diagnostic instrument to assess students' engagement with existential thought. Educators can use the results to:

- **Identify students** with high existential intelligence who may benefit from more advanced discussions.

- **Tailor lesson plans** to foster deeper reflection in students struggling with abstract thinking.

By integrating existential intelligence into the curriculum, educators empower students to engage with life's profound questions, cultivate critical thinking skills, and develop a sense of purpose.

This not only enhances the learning experience but also prepares students to navigate an increasingly complex and interconnected world with confidence and intellectual curiosity.

Technological Integration and Existential Intelligence

The Role of Technology in Existential Exploration

Existential intelligence involves deep reflection on fundamental life questions, such as:

- What is the meaning of life?
- What is the nature of reality?
- What happens after death?
- How do we define morality and justice?

Traditionally, existential inquiry has been explored through philosophy, religion, literature, and the arts (Gardner, 1999). However, in the modern era, digital technologies provide new, interactive, and immersive ways to engage with these profound questions (Gee, 2007; McGonigal, 2011).

This chapter examines:

1. How digital tools, games, and virtual reality enhance existential intelligence by creating experiences that promote deep reflection.

2. The challenges posed by digital culture—how the fast-paced, distraction-heavy nature of modern technology can undermine deep existential thought.

3. Practical strategies for integrating technology while preserving meaningful existential inquiry, particularly in educational settings.

By exploring the intersection of technology and existential intelligence, this chapter ensures that existential inquiry remains relevant, engaging, and accessible in the digital age.

Digital Tools for Enhancing Existential Intelligence

Technological advancements have expanded the ways individuals interact with profound questions about life, reality, and human existence. Below are key digital tools that enhance existential intelligence.

Virtual Reality (VR) and Immersive Experiences

Virtual reality (VR) is increasingly being used as a transformative tool for existential exploration. VR allows users to step into new realities, experience alternative perspectives, and engage with abstract existential themes (Slater & Sanchez-Vives, 2016).

Examples of VR Experiences for Existential Exploration:

- **VR Space Exploration and the Cosmic Perspective** – Apps like Universe Sandbox and Titans of Space allow users to experience the vastness of the cosmos, fostering awe, existential humility, and deep reflection on humanity's place in the universe (Yaden et al., 2016).

- **VR Experiences of Different Life Perspectives** – Programs like Be Another Lab enable users to experience life from another person's perspective, enhancing empathy and philosophical reflection on human identity and consciousness (Banakou, Groten, & Slater, 2013).

- **Meditation and Mindfulness VR** – Apps like TRIPP and Guided Meditation VR help users detach from distractions and engage in deep self-reflection and meaning-making.

Implication: VR can serve as a powerful tool for engaging with existential questions, making abstract philosophical discussions tangible and immersive.

Philosophical and Narrative-Based Video Games

Video games have evolved beyond mere entertainment into interactive storytelling experiences that engage players in deep existential reflection (Bogost, 2010; Sicart, 2013).

Examples of Games That Explore Existential Themes:

- The Stanley Parable (2013) – Explores free will, determinism, and the illusion of choice through interactive storytelling (Anthropy & Clark, 2014).

- Journey (2012) – Uses symbolism and an emotional narrative to represent life as a metaphorical journey, evoking themes of companionship, solitude, and transcendence (McGonigal, 2011).

- The Witness (2016) – Features mystery and environmental storytelling to explore consciousness, perception, and the search for meaning (Blow, 2016).

- NieR: Automata (2017) – Examines existential dread, artificial intelligence, and the nature of human existence (Takahashi, 2017).

Implication: Well-designed games can act as modern philosophical playgrounds, engaging players in existential dilemmas through experiential learning rather than traditional instruction.

Artificial Intelligence and Chatbots for Philosophical Inquiry

AI-driven chatbots and conversational agents, such as ChatGPT and Socratic AI tutors, can facilitate deep discussions on existential topics (Russell & Norvig, 2021).

Applications in Existential Intelligence:

- **AI-Powered Socratic Dialogue** – Chatbots designed to challenge beliefs, ask thought-provoking questions, and explore philosophical ideas interactively (Colton, López de Mántaras, & Stock, 2009).

- **AI-Assisted Reflective Writing** – AI tools that analyze essays or journals, providing feedback on the depth and coherence of existential arguments (Bender & Koller, 2020).

- **AI Ethics Simulations** – Platforms that allow users to engage in ethical dilemmas and explore existential questions about morality and consciousness (Moor, 2006).

Implication: AI can serve as a reflective tool, prompting new perspectives and critical thinking on existential matters.

Challenges of Technology in Existential Reflection

While technology provides new opportunities for existential intelligence, it also introduces challenges that must be carefully managed.

Digital Distractions and Superficial Engagement

Constant exposure to social media, notifications, and digital entertainment can diminish the depth of reflection, replacing meaningful existential inquiry with superficial content consumption.

Solution: Encourage "digital minimalism" and intentional technology use—students should balance screen time with deep, uninterrupted reflection.

Existential Anxiety in the Digital Age

Exposure to rapidly evolving AI, global crises, and existential threats (e.g., climate change, automation) through digital media may heighten existential anxiety rather than deepen existential intelligence.

Solution: Implement digital well-being strategies, such as reflective journaling or guided philosophical discussions, to help individuals process and contextualize existential fears in a constructive way.

Echo Chambers and Confirmation Bias

The personalized algorithms of social media can trap individuals in intellectual echo chambers, limiting exposure to diverse existential perspectives.

Solution: Educators and students should actively seek diverse viewpoints, exploring philosophies, cultures, and perspectives beyond their digital bubbles.

Strategies for Integrating Technology into Existential Intelligence Development

To harness technology effectively while minimizing its drawbacks, educators and learners can adopt the following strategies:

Mindful Use of Digital Tools

- Introduce structured VR experiences that promote existential reflection.

- Encourage students to play philosophical video games and discuss their themes.

- Use AI-based chatbots for Socratic dialogue and critical thinking exercises.

Digital Detox and Reflective Practices

- Designate tech-free periods for deep self-reflection and philosophical inquiry.

- Implement journaling assignments where students reflect on existential questions without digital interference.

Expanding Philosophical Literacy through Technology

- Introduce students to online archives of philosophical works (e.g., Stanford Encyclopedia of Philosophy).

- Use interactive AI-driven platforms to simulate debates between historical philosophers.

Technology as a Gateway to Existential Exploration

Technology, when used intentionally, can serve as a powerful enabler of existential intelligence, providing individuals with new ways to explore, reflect, and engage with profound questions. However, thoughtful integration is essential to prevent distraction, anxiety, and intellectual stagnation.

By balancing digital engagement with deep reflection, educators and learners can leverage technological advancements to enrich existential inquiry, ensuring that the search for meaning remains central in an increasingly digital world.

Final Considerations

Throughout this book, we have explored existential intelligence as a distinctive and profound dimension of human cognition—one that transcends traditional intelligence frameworks and delves into fundamental questions of existence, purpose, and meaning. As we have seen, existential intelligence is not merely a philosophical abstraction but a cognitive faculty that shapes decision-making, emotional resilience, and personal fulfillment.

By examining the theoretical foundations of existential intelligence, we have traced its historical and cultural significance, distinguishing it from spiritual intelligence while acknowledging its intersections with philosophy, neuroscience, and psychology. The empirical studies reviewed in this book underscore the growing interest in this domain, particularly regarding its assessment and application across diverse contexts. The development of new psychometric instruments, as proposed herein, represents a crucial step toward formalizing existential intelligence within the broader framework of multiple intelligences.

The practical implications of existential intelligence are far-reaching. In education, fostering existential inquiry can help students develop critical thinking and ethical reasoning, equipping them to navigate an increasingly complex and uncertain world. In professional and organizational settings, existential intelligence can enhance leadership, ethical decision-making, and overall workplace well-being. Moreover, as society grapples with challenges such as environmental crises, technological disruptions, and sociopolitical instability, existential intelligence offers a means to cultivate resilience, adaptability, and a deeper sense of purpose.

Despite these promising directions, existential intelligence remains an evolving field of study. Further research is needed to refine assessment methodologies, uncover its neurological underpinnings, and explore its potential applications in mental health, education, and public policy. Additionally, as artificial intelligence continues to reshape human cognition and labor markets, existential intelligence may prove to be an essential skill for preserving human identity and agency in a rapidly changing world.

Ultimately, this book serves as an invitation for continued exploration and dialogue. By recognizing the significance of existential intelligence, we can foster a culture that values deep reflection, ethical inquiry, and a holistic understanding of human potential. In a world marked by volatility and complexity, the ability to engage meaningfully with life's most profound questions is not only an intellectual pursuit but a necessity for both personal and collective well-being.

As we move forward, let us embrace the challenge of integrating existential intelligence into our educational systems, professional environments, and daily lives. By doing so, we can empower individuals and communities to seek meaning, cultivate wisdom, and navigate the uncertainties of existence with clarity and purpose.

Bibliographic References

1. **ABIMBOLA, W.** *Ifá: An Exposition of Ifá Literary Corpus.* Oxford University Press, 1976.

2. **ALEXANDER, N. M. C.; COLUCI, M. Z. O.** "Content Validity in the Processes of Construction and Adaptation of Measurement Instruments." *Science & Collective Health*, vol. 7, 2011, pp. 3061-3068.

3. **ALLAN, B. A.; SHEARER, B.** "The Scale for Existential Thinking." *International Journal of Transpersonal Studies*, vol. 31, no. 1, 2012, pp. 21-37.

4. **ALLMAN, J. M., et al.** "The Anterior Cingulate Cortex: The Evolution of an Interface Between Emotion and Cognition." *The New York Academy of Sciences*, vol. 935, no. 1, 2006, pp. 107-117. Available at: https://doi.org/10.1111/j.1749-6632.2001.tb03476.x. Accessed 12 Sept. 2023.

5. **ANDRADE, R. R.; SMITH, M. F. M. D. S.; GOMES, R. L. R.** "On the Experience of Meaning at Work and in Organizations: Contributions of Logotherapy and Existential Analysis." *Revista Contribuciones a las Ciencias Sociales*, São José dos Pinhais, vol. 16, no. 7, 2023, pp. 6407-6427.

6. **ANTHROPY, A.; CLARK, N.** *A Game Design Vocabulary: Exploring the Foundations of Experiences in Video Games.* Pearson Education, 2014.

7. **AQUINO, T. D.** *Summa Theologica.* 5th ed., Loyola Editions, vol. 1, 2001.

8. **ARISTOTLE.** *Nicomachean Ethics.* 350 BCE.

9. **ASTUTI, S. A.; LAKO, A.; UTAMI, M. S. S.** "Existential Intelligence and Pro-Environmental Behavior of Students in Adiwiyata and Non-Adiwiyata Schools: Are They Different?" *Journal of Southwest Jiaotong University*, vol. 56, no. 6, 2021. Available at: https://doi.org/10.35741/issn.0258-2724.56.6.62. Accessed 12 Sept. 2023.

10. **AYASRAH, S. M.; ALJARRAH, A. H.** "The Differences in Multiple Intelligences Between the Students of Jordan University of Science and Technology." *International Journal of Higher Education*, vol. 9, no. 4, 2020. Available at: https://doi.org/10.5430/ijhe.v9n4p35. Accessed 12 Sept. 2023.

11. **BANAKOU, D.; GROTEN, R.; SLATER, M.** "Illusory Ownership of a Virtual Child Body Causes Overestimation of Object Sizes and Implicit Attitude Changes." *Proceedings of the National Academy of Sciences*, vol. 110, no. 31, 2013, pp. 12846-12851.

12. **BATTISTE, M.** *Indigenous Knowledge and Pedagogy in First Nations Education: A Literature Review with Recommendations.*, 2002.

13. **BENDER, E. M.; KOLLER, A.** "Climbing Towards NLU: On Meaning, Form, and Understanding in the Age of Data." *Proceedings of the 58th Annual Meeting of the Association for Computational Linguistics*, 2020.

14. **BLOW, J.** *The Witness: Game Design and Philosophy.* Thekla Inc., 2016.

15. **BOGOST, I.** *Persuasive Games: The Expressive Power of Videogames.* MIT Press, 2010.

16. **BOSS, J. A.** "The Autonomy of Moral Intelligence." *Educational Theory*, vol. 44, no. 4, 2005, pp. 399-416.

17. **BRANCHES, D. K.; MARTINS, P. N.** "Digital Games in Educational Contexts and Multiple Intelligences: Approaches and Contributions to Learning." *Research, Society and Development*, vol. 7, no. 5, 2018, pp. 01-17.

18. **BRANCUCCI, A., et al.** "The Sound of Consciousness: Neural Underpinnings of Auditory Perception." *Journal of Neuroscience*, vol. 31, no. 46, 2011, pp. 16611-16618.

19. **BÜHNER, M.; KRÖNER, S.; ZIEGLER, M.** "Working Memory, Visual–Spatial Intelligence, and Their Relationship to Problem-Solving." *Intelligence*, vol. 36, no. 6, 2008, pp. 672-680. Available at: https://doi.org/10.1016/j.intell.2008.03.008. Accessed 12 Sept. 2023.

20. **CAMUS, A.** *State of Siege; The Foreigner.* Translation by Maria Jacintha and Antônio Quadros. São Paulo: Abril Cultural, 1979.

21. **CAMUS, A.** *The Myth of Sisyphus.* 1942.

22. **CAMUS, A.** *The Myth of Sisyphus.* Translation by Ari Roitman and Paulina Watch. Rio de Janeiro: Record, 2004.

23. **COLOM, R., et al.** "Human Intelligence and Brain Networks." *Dialogues in Clinical Neuroscience*, vol. 12, no. 4, 2010, pp. 489-501.

24. **COLTON, S.; LÓPES DE MÁNTARAS, R.; STOCK, O.** *"Computational Creativity: Coming of Age."* AI Magazine, vol. 30, no. 3, 2009, pp. 11-24.

25. **CRICK, F.; CLARK, J.** "The Astonishing Hypothesis." *Journal of Consciousness Studies*, vol. 1, no. 1, 1994, pp. 10-16.

26. **DALAI LAMA.** *The Art of Happiness.* 1999.

27. **ELIADE, M.** *Patterns in Comparative Religion.* 1958.

28. **FERNANDES, S. J.** "Existential Intelligence Scale and its Implications for Preliminary Assessment of Ontological Insecurity." *PsyArXiv*, 2021. Available at: https://doi.org/10.31234/osf.io/8e5kq. Accessed 12 Sept. 2023.

29. **FERRERO, M.; VADILLO, M. A.; LÉON, S. P.** "A Valid Evaluation of the Theory of Multiple Intelligences is Not Yet Possible: Problems of Methodological Quality for

Intervention Studies." *Intelligence*, vol. 88, 2021. Available at: https://doi.org/10.1016/j.intell.2021.101566.

30. **FORSYTHE, J.; MONGRAIN, M.** "The Existential Nihilism Scale (ENS): Theory, Development, and Psychometric Evaluation." *Journal of Psychopathology and Behavioral Assessment*, vol. 45, 2023, pp. 865-883. Available at: https://doi.org/10.1007/s10862-023-10052-w. Accessed 12 Sept. 2023.

31. **FRANKL, V. E.** *In Search of Meaning: A Psychologist in the Concentration Camp.* Synodal Press, vol. 3, 2013.

32. **FRIEDMAN, D.; NESSLER, D.; JOHNSON JR, R.** "Memory Encoding and Retrieval in the Aging Brain." *Neurobiology of Aging*, vol. 38, no. 1, 2007, pp. 2-7.

33. **GANIS, G.; THOMPSON, W. L.; KOSSLYN, S. M.** "Brain Areas Underlying Visual Mental Imagery and Visual Perception: An fMRI Study." *Cognitive Brain Research*, vol. 20, no. 2, 2004.

34. **GARDNER, H.** *Frames of Mind: The Theory of Multiple Intelligences.* Basic Books, 1983.

35. **GARDNER, H.** *Frames of Mind: The Theory of Multiple Intelligences.* 10th anniversary ed., Basic Books, 1993.

36. **GARDNER, H.** *The Disciplined Mind: What All Students Should Understand.* Simon & Schuster, 1999.

37. **GARDNER, H.** "A Case Against Spiritual Intelligence." *The International Journal for the Psychology of Religion,*

vol. 1, no. 10, 2000, pp. 27-34. Available at: https://doi.org/10.1207/S15327582IJPR1001_3. Accessed 12 Sept. 2023.

38. **GARDNER, H.** *Howard Gardner Under Fire: The Rebel Psychologist Faces His Critics.* Open Court, 2006, pp. 277-344.

39. **GARDNER, H.** *Multiple Intelligences: New Horizons.* Basic Books, 2006.

40. **GARDNER, H.** "A Resurgence of Interest in Existential Intelligence: Why Now?" *Howard Gardner*, 2020. Available at: https://www.howardgardner.com/howards-blog/a-resurgence-of-interest-in-existential-intelligence-why-now. Accessed 12 Sept. 2023.

41. **GEE, J. P.** *What Video Games Have to Teach Us About Learning and Literacy.* Palgrave Macmillan, 2007.

42. **GOLEMAN, D.** *Emotional Intelligence.* Bantam Books, 1995.

43. **GORIOUNOVA, N. A.; MANSVELDER, H. D.** "Genes, Cells, and Brain Areas of Intelligence." *Frontiers in Human Neuroscience*, vol. 13, 2019. Available at: https://doi.org/10.3389/fnhum.2019.00044. Accessed 12 Sept. 2023.

44. **HEIDEGGER, M.** *Being and Time.* Vozes, vol. 1, 1988.

45. **JADDOU, E. A. A.** "Existential Intelligence Among Graduate Students at the World Islamic Sciences University

in Jordan." *Academic Journals*, vol. 13, no. 3, 10 July 2018, pp. 534-542.

46. **JOURNEY Through the Timeline.** *Becoming Human*, 2023. Available at: https://becominghuman.org/timeline/. Accessed 11 Sept. 2023.

47. **KIERKEGAARD, S.** *Fear and Trembling and The Sickness Unto Death.* Princeton University Press, 2013.

48. **KORNHABER, M.; FIERROS, E.; VEENEMA, S.** *Multiple Intelligences: Best Ideas from Research and Practice.* Pearson Education Inc, 2004.

49. **LYNN, M. R.** "Determination and Quantification of Content Validity." *Nursing Research*, vol. 35, no. 6, 1986, pp. 382-385.

50. **MACKENZIE, W.** *Multiple Intelligences Inventory.* Surfaquarium, 1999. Available at: https://surfaquarium.com/MI/inventory.htm. Accessed 11 Sept. 2023.

51. **MASLOW, A.** "A Theory of Human Motivation." 1943.

52. **MBITI, J.** *African Religions and Philosophy.* 1969.

53. **MCGONIGAL, J.** *Reality is Broken: Why Games Make Us Better and How They Can Change the World.* Penguin, 2011.

54. **MOOR, J. H.** "The Nature, Importance, and Difficulty of Machine Ethics." *IEEE Intelligent Systems*, vol. 21, no. 4, 2006, pp. 18-21.

55. **NEDELCU, E.** "Consumerism Versus the Culture of Existential Intelligence." *Romanian Review of Social Sciences*, vol. 12, no. 1, 2021, pp. 3-15.

56. **NEISSER, U., et al.** "Intelligence: Knowns and Unknowns." *American Psychologist*, vol. 51, no. 2, 1996, pp. 77-101. Available at: https://doi.org/10.1037/0003-066X.51.2.77. Accessed 12 Sept. 2023.

57. **NISBETT, R.** *The Geography of Thought: How Asians and Westerners Think Differently...and Why.* 2003.

58. **PARAMASIVAM, T., et al.** "Existential Intelligence Influences Adversity Quotient Among Youth in Becoming Life Smart Learner." *Journal of Pharmaceutical Negative Results*, vol. 13, no. 9, 2022, pp. 5978-5991.

59. **PIAGET, J.** *The Psychology of Intelligence.* London: Routledge, 1950.

60. **PIAGET, J.** *The Origins of Intelligence in Children.* International Universities Press, New York, 1952.

61. **PLATO.** *Republic.* c. 375 BCE.

62. **RADHAKRISHNAN, S., & MOORE, C. A.** *A Sourcebook in Indian Philosophy.* 1957.

63. **RAHULA, W.** *What the Buddha Taught.* 1974.

64. **RODRIGUES, F. D. A. A.** "Intelligence DWRI." *Recisatec – Scientific Journal of Health and Technology*, vol. 2, no. 12, Dec. 2022. Available at:

https://doi.org/10.53612/recisatec.v2i12.232. Accessed 12 Sept. 2023.

65. **RODRIGUES, F. D. A.; WAGNER, R. E. S.; BARTH, N.** "General Intelligence." *Latin Science Multidisciplinary Scientific Journal*, vol. 6, no. 1, 2022, pp. 4990-4998.

66. **RUSSELL, B.** *A History of Western Philosophy.* 1945.

67. **RUSSELL, S. J., & NORVIG, P.** *Artificial Intelligence: A Modern Approach* (4th ed.). Pearson, 2021.

68. **SANTOS, R. O. D.** "Structure and Functions of the Cerebral Cortex." Faculty of Health Sciences of the University Center of Brasília, Brasília, 2002.

69. **SARTRE, J.-P.** *Being and Nothingness.* Book Sales, 1982.

70. **SCOPI.** "Mundo VUCA e BANI." 24 Feb. 2023. Available at:
https://scopi.com.br/blog/mundo-vuca-e-bani/#:~:text=Mundo%20VUCA%20e%20BANI%20s%C3%A3o,forma%20como%20as%20organiza%C3%A7%C3%B5es%20atuam. Accessed 11 Sept. 2023.

71. **SHARMA, A.; JHA, A.** "Who Are We As Humans?: A Question Raised By Existential Intelligence." *Meri Journal of Education*, vol. XVII, no. 1, April 2022.

72. **SHARMA, A.; JHA, A. K.** "Existential Intelligence Among University Students Attributed to Gender and Study Level of Participants." *Education India Journal: A Quarterly*

Refereed Journal of Dialogues on Education, vol. 10, no. 1, 2021, pp. 113-122.

73. **SICART, M.** *Beyond Choices: The Design of Ethical Gameplay.* MIT Press, 2013.

74. **SKRZYPIŃSKA, K.** "Does Spiritual Intelligence (SI) Exist? A Theoretical Investigation of a Tool Useful for Finding the Meaning of Life." *Journal of Religion and Health*, vol. 60, no. 1, Feb. 2021, pp. 500-516. Available at: https://link.springer.com/article/10.1007/s10943-020-01005-8. Accessed 11 Sept. 2023.

75. **SLATER, M., & SANCHEZ-VIVES, M. V.** "Enhancing Our Lives with Immersive Virtual Reality." *Frontiers in Robotics and AI*, vol. 3, no. 74, 2016.

76. **SPENCER, J. L., et al.** "Uncovering the Mechanisms of Estrogen Effects on Hippocampal Function." *Frontiers in Neuroendocrinology*, vol. 2, 2008, pp. 219-237.

77. **STADLER, M., et al.** "Complex Problem Solving and Intelligence: A Meta-Analysis." *Intelligence*, vol. 53, 2015, pp. 92-101. Available at: https://doi.org/10.1016/j.intell.2015.09.005. Accessed 12 Sept. 2023.

78. **SUZUKI, D. T.** *Zen Buddhism.* 1956.

79. **TAFNER, M. A.** "Artificial Neural Networks: How the Nervous System Works." *Brain & Mind*, Mar/May 1998. Available at:

https://cerebromente.org.br/n05/tecnologia/nervoso.htm. Accessed 11 Sept. 2023.

80. **TAKAHASHI, D.** "NieR: Automata and the Philosophy of AI Consciousness." *GameSpot Interviews*, 2017.

81. **TURKEN, U. A.; WHITFIELD-GABRIELI, S.; BAMMER, R.** "Cognitive Processing Speed and the Structure of White Matter Pathways: Convergent Evidence from Normal Variation and Lesion Studies." *NeuroImage*, vol. 42, 2008, pp. 1032-1044.

82. **YADEN, D. B., et al.** "The overview effect: Awe and self-transcendent experience in space flight.*"Psychology of Consciousness: Theory, Research, and Practice"*, vol. 3, no. 1, 2016, pp. 1-11.

83. **ZAMROZIEWICZ, M. K., et al.** "Parahippocampal Cortex Mediates the Relationship Between Lutein and Crystallized Intelligence in Healthy, Older Adults." *Frontiers in Aging Neuroscience*, vol. 8, 2016. Available at: https://doi.org/10.3389/fnagi.2016.00297. Accessed 12 Sept. 2023.

84. **ZUBI, A.; AL-RABEE, F.; AL-JARRAH, N. A.** "Intuitive Intelligence and Its Relation to Gender Variators and the Academic Level: A Field Study on a Sample of the Faculty of Education Students." *Journal of the Islamic University for Educational and Psychological Studies*, vol. 23, no. 3, 2015, pp. 129-145.